PLUTARCH:
LIVES OF GALBA & OTHO

PLUTARCH:
LIVES OF GALBA & OTHO

A Companion

Translation and Commentary by
Douglas Little and Christopher Ehrhardt

Bristol Classical Press

This impression 2008
First published in 1994 by
Bristol Classical Press
an imprint of
Gerald Duckworth & Co. Ltd.
90-93 Cowcross Street, London EC1M 6BF
Tel: 020 7490 7300
Fax: 020 7490 0080
info@duckworth-publishers.co.uk
www.ducknet.co.uk

A catalogue record for this book is available
from the British Library

ISBN 978 1 85399 429 6

Contents

Acknowledgements

Writing the Commentary on these *Lives* by Plutarch would have been impossible if the University of Otago had not granted me short leave in 1992. An invitation from Professor Peter Franke enabled me to work uninterruptedly in the Institute for Ancient History at the University of the Saarland, Saarbrücken, and Dr Manfred Wörrle gave me unrestricted access to the facilities of the Kommission für Alte Geschichte und Epigraphik in Munich. Their generosity, and the unstinting help I received while in Germany, made it possible for me to work through the secondary literature, much of which is inaccessible in New Zealand, and to bring the Bibliography up to date, to early 1992. If the Commentary has any value, it is very largely due to them; the faults remain my own.

C.E.

The translation, and the comments on it in the Introduction, were written by Douglas Little, the Commentary, and the rest of the Introduction, by Christopher Ehrhardt.

D.L.

Introduction

1. Plutarch and his Work

Plutarch's most famous and popular work is his *Parallel Lives*, the paired biographies of famous Greeks and Romans. Apart from these twenty-two surviving pairs of biographies (at least one further pair is lost), four other *Lives* by Plutarch survive, of Artaxerxes II (king of Persia, 404-359 BC), of Aratus (a Greek politician of the third century BC), and of two Roman emperors, Galba and Otho. These last two formed part of a series of the lives of the early emperors, from Augustus to Vitellius, of which all the others are lost, except for a few short quotations. It seems, however, that they formed a continuous history of the Roman emperors up to AD 69: certainly the narrative is continuous from the end of *Galba* into *Otho*, so that there is no description of the character and background of the new emperor in the *Otho*, since this had already been given in the biography of Galba.

The events of AD 68 and early 69, described in these two lives, took place when Plutarch was a young man, and he in fact provides the earliest detailed account of the overthrow of Nero and the accessions and deaths of his first two successors.

Plutarch's exact date of birth is not known, but in one of his essays about Delphi (*On the E at Delphi* 1, *Moralia* 385B) he says that he was a student of Ammonius at Athens at the time of Nero's visit to Greece, in AD 66-67. Since he must have been at least sixteen or seventeen then, he was born at the latest in AD 50; on the other hand, since he was still active in the 120s he is not likely to have been born before about AD 40. So he was in his late teens or twenties when Nero committed suicide and Galba was proclaimed emperor.

Plutarch was a native of Chaeronea, a small town in Boeotia, the region of central Greece bordering on Attica. Despite his extensive travels and the wide renown he gained in later life, he always looked on Chaeronea as his home, and was unwilling, by moving away, to decrease its population, even though his studies were hampered by the fact that there was no library there to compare with those at Athens or at Rome (*Demosthenes* 2). His family was well established and prosperous, and continued to flourish for over two

1

centuries after Plutarch's death. Probably in his twenties he married Timoxena, who bore him four sons and a daughter; two of the boys died young, and the death of the daughter at the age of two was the occasion for Plutarch's moving letter of consolation to his wife (*Moralia* 608-12).

Plutarch obviously received a good education in literature and rhetoric before he went to Athens to study under the philosopher Ammonius, through whose influence he became a convinced Platonist. He was granted Athenian citizenship, perhaps while still a student; later, either under Vespasian (AD 69-79) or under Domitian (AD 81-96), he also received Roman citizenship, through his patron Mestrius Florus, a friend of Vespasian's, who was suffect consul in one of the years between AD 72 and 75. Plutarch visited the battlefield of Bedriacum, where Otho's army had been defeated in the civil war by the Vitellian forces, with Mestrius, and heard his reminiscences of the battle (*Otho* 14).

Plutarch's writings make it plain that, as well as his native Boeotia, he knew Athens and Delphi well and had travelled widely in other parts of Greece. He had probably visited Asia Minor (*Moralia* 501E), and certainly Alexandria (*Moralia* 678C), which may have been the home of his teacher Ammonius. He travelled in Italy several times from the 70s on and knew Rome well, but only began to study Latin literature late in life and never knew the language well enough to venture on literary criticism (*Demosthenes* 2).

A few of Plutarch's philosophical writings refer to contemporary political conditions, most notably the essay, *Precepts of Statecraft* (*Moralia* 798-825), in which he advises a young friend about the possibilities and limits of political activity in a Greek city-state under Roman rule, but his chief interest and source of inspiration was always the classical age of Greece, from the semi-mythical times of Lycurgus, who was credited with establishing the 'good order' of the Spartan political system, to the age of the successors of Alexander the Great, and he draws the great majority of his examples from these centuries which, seen from the perspective of small-town life under the Roman empire, had the glamour of an heroic and golden age. Similarly, Plutarch's literary quotations, with which his works are full, come above all from Homer, and otherwise mostly from authors who had died three centuries or more before he was born. It is therefore very remarkable that he turned to writing recent political history, in his series of imperial biographies. Unfortunately both the beginning and the end of this series – the *Lives* of Augustus and of Vitellius – are lost, so we do not have his explanation of his reasons.

2

2. Date and sources of the *Galba* and *Otho*

The chronology of Plutarch's works is an unsolved and probably insoluble problem, but it seems likely that most of those which survive were written after the assassination of the emperor Domitian in AD 96, when Plutarch was probably in his late 40s. However, the *Galba* and *Otho*, and their lost companions in the series of imperial lives, ending with the *Life* of Vitellius, may well have been written under Domitian. The *Vitellius* must have ended with Vitellius' death and the proclamation of Vespasian who, like a second Augustus, brought peace and stability after the horrors of civil war. This would be a suitable place to end the series, if it was written under Domitian, and explain why it went no further – it was not politic to write the history of the reigning dynasty. Similarly both Tacitus (cf. *H.* I 1 fin.) and Suetonius took care not to extend their historical and biographical works into the time of the dynasty founded by Nerva and continued, through adoptions, by Trajan and Hadrian, under whom they wrote. If these *Lives* were indeed written under Domitian, then they must have been completed and published before AD 93, the year in which Junius Mauricus, whom Plutarch calls 'a man who deserved his high reputation' (*Galba* 8.8), was exiled and his brother Arulenus was executed for treason (Tac. *Agr.* 45.1). In that case Plutarch was writing only some twenty years after the events. He had no direct knowledge of them, since it is practically certain that he was not in Italy in AD 68-69, but he could get information from contemporaries and even eye-witnesses.

However, it is clear that for much of his narrative Plutarch depends on an earlier written and published account. This is proved by the close similarity of much of his narrative to those of our other main sources, Tacitus' *Histories*, and Suetonius' *Lives* of Nero, Galba and Otho (the *History* of Dio Cassius survives only in excerpts by Byzantine writers, but also seems to have followed the same tradition), while the differences between these accounts show that none of these writers was drawing on any other of the surviving accounts. The identity of this lost source has been sought with much effort and ingenuity for the past century and a half, but there is still no general agreement, above all because the various possibilities are only names to us, with, at most, only a few sentences of their works still surviving in quotations by extant writers. The source will therefore be called the 'Common Source' in the following discussion and in the Commentary.

Plutarch himself mentions no source by name in the *Galba*; in the *Otho* he mentions two, Cluvius Rufus (*Otho* 3.2) and (Julius) Secundus (*Otho* 9.3), as well as anonymous sources, which may have been written or oral (*Otho* 9.1, 3, 14.1). Of these, Cluvius Rufus is fairly well known: he was a leading senator and ex-consul, whose consulship perhaps was earlier than AD 41;[1]

he was prominent at Nero's court (Suet. *Nero* 21.2; Tac. *H*. IV 43), and distinguished by literary and forensic ability. Galba appointed him governor of Spain, probably of all three provinces; after Galba's murder he gave his allegiance to Vitellius, went to join him in Gaul and accompanied him on his march to Italy (Tac. *H*. I 8, 76, II 65). In December of 69 he was one of the two senators present at Vitellius' attempt to abdicate (Tac. *H*. III 65); his date of death is unknown, but he survived for at least some years after 69, and probably wrote his historical work in Vespasian's reign (cf. Pliny, *Ep*. IX 19.5).

Little is known of Julius Secundus, since it is only conjecture which identifies the Secundus whom Plutarch mentions as a rhetorician and secretary *ab epistulis* to Otho with the Julius Secundus who was a friend of Quintilian and died in the 80s AD (Quintilian, *Institutio Oratoria* X 1, 120), and who appears as a character in Tacitus' *Dialogue on Orators*. If the identification is correct, then Secundus was an equestrian from Gaul, distinguished for eloquence, which no doubt was one motive for Otho's choice of him to take charge of his official correspondence. Plutarch quotes him only as authority for the opinion that Otho hastened on the decisive battle at Bedriacum through his own impatience, and there is no reason to believe that Secundus wrote a full account even of the battle, let alone of the reigns of Galba and Otho together; more probably his opinion was one of several quoted by the 'Common Source'.

Several other names have been suggested for the 'Common Source', among them the elder Pliny, Fabius Rusticus, and Vipstanus Messalla. All of these are discussed, briefly and incisively, by Syme (*Tacitus* 674-6), who also introduces the possibility of a work by Marius Celsus (ibid. and 683), but wisely concludes, 'It is safer to confess ignorance'. No later discussions have produced evidence or cogent arguments to alter this decision, though C.P. Jones, *Plutarch and Rome* 75-8, gives a refreshingly unorthodox but rather improbable defence of Plutarch's originality. The latest discussion, by M. Sage, *ANRW* II 33, 22, 893-7, again states the case for the elder Pliny as the main source, which had already been made, with care and insight, by Fabia in 1893.

3. Literary sources for the Reigns of Galba and Otho

Besides Tacitus' *Histories*, as parallel accounts for the events which Plutarch describes we have Suetonius' *Lives* of the first twelve emperors, of which of course the *Lives* of Galba and Otho, along with parts of those of Nero and of Vitellius, are the most relevant; the Byzantine summaries and quotations from the *Roman History* of Dio Cassius, and earliest of all, the rapid summary by Josephus, *Jewish War* IV 491-6, who states (496, cf. 440) that even when he wrote (in the 70s), 'these events had been written up by many of the Greeks and Romans'.

The only English commentary on these two *Lives* was written by E.G. Hardy, for school use, and published in 1890; despite its age and different purpose, it has been of outstanding value in composing this one. Unfortunately the edition of the *Galba*, with translation and commentary in modern Greek, by Alexander I. Kessissoglu (Athens, 1984), was not available to us.

4. The Translation[2]

A true translation should express the meaning of the original accurately, and mirror the individuality of the author's style. This is the ideal which Jacques Amyot, Plutarch's first great European translator, set before himself: 'The office of a fit translater, consisteth not onely in the faithfull expressing of his authors meaning, but also in a certaine resembling and shadowing out of the forme of his style and the manner of his speaking'.[3] In translating the *Lives* Amyot did not find it easy to satisfy these demands, and he admits that 'men (may) find not the speech of this translation so flowing, as they have found some other of mine'.[4]

The difficulties were two-fold. The first, which Amyot does not mention – I suppose he would have taken it as self-evident – is not peculiar to Plutarch but intrinsic to translation from Greek to any language such as French or English. Meaning in Greek is in essence independent of word-order, which is therefore extremely flexible; and while this flexibility is, in the hands of a good Greek writer, a fertile source of emphasis and variety, for Amyot, or us, to reproduce the effect may be virtually impossible.

The second difficulty was Plutarch's complex style – what Amyot calls 'Plutarkes peculiar manner of inditing' – which made his Greek hard to understand, let alone represent in all its nuances. Hence Amyot claims for his work only the very modest merit that even experts will find it simpler than the original: 'How harsh or rude soever my speech be, yet am I sure that my translation will be much easier to my contriemen, than the Greeke copie is, even to such as are best practised in the Greeke tonge'.[5]

Now in theory, Plutarch placed little weight on style – it was content that mattered, not the way it was expressed – but both the words he uses and the way he structures them bear a highly personal stamp.

His mind was a storehouse of the literature of eight centuries, and he draws deeply on this rich resource as well as on the vernacular of his own time. Thus the range of his vocabulary is extremely wide. He uses many words either rare in themselves, or in senses which are rare. He apparently coins words himself, and has a fondness, which he shares with his contemporaries, for abstract terms and words in unusual compound form. His sentences, reflecting his leisurely and discursive narrative, seem to move with the artless negligence of after-dinner conversation. It is as if they grow spontaneously, as one idea, then another, suggests itself to the writer's mind, and they are often, like the loose accretions of conversation, long, circuitous, and heavy-loaded.

Ziegler, whose own style gives some notion of Plutarch's, describes the complex structures which typically result from this expansiveness: 'Long-drawn out periods, expanded by numerous subordinate clauses and participial interpolations, not infrequently interrupted by rather lengthy parentheses, are characteristic of Plutarch's unhurried narrative style'.[6] Ziegler's comment on the intelligibility of these periods is notable for its restraint: they are 'on the whole', he says, 'transparent, generally speaking'; one is not surprised when he adds, 'they call for an attentive reader'.[7]

If there were no more to it than that, they would also call for an attentive translator, but Plutarch, despite his theoretical position and his appearance of negligence, is far from artless. No one who was educated in his time could be indifferent to style; education was based on literature, and meant, in its highest form, the study of rhetoric – that is, the art of speaking and writing well. To ignore the expectations of one's audience would have been an astonishing eccentricity in the Graeco-Roman world, and Plutarch's regard for accepted formalities is clear. Greeks, even when reading alone, normally read aloud, and aural harmony was a vital component of style. Plutarch carefully avoids hiatus,[8] and although his sentences may meander, their structure is not haphazard. They regularly end in one of the four cadences most commonly used in Greek artistic prose and so, often, do the major units within them.

English prose has its own rhythms, and these can supply the effect of Plutarch's cadences, but his avoidance of hiatus creates a more difficult problem. A Greek sentence may be flexible in its word-order, but it is not arbitrary; its parts are related in patterns which enable a reader to anticipate the connections of thought. In avoiding hiatus, however, Plutarch often disrupts these patterns, and it is this as much as anything that leads Amyot to speak of his 'crabbed roughness'. It is as if one is looking at a mosaic in which some of the pieces have been deliberately displaced.

The difficulty which translators have felt in doing justice to Plutarch's leisurely, yet rich and complex style, can be judged by their reaction to the efforts of their colleagues. Amyot had tried faithfully to reproduce the run of Plutarch's sentences; North (who translated Amyot, not the original) often feels obliged to break up Amyot's French. Dryden, under whose name a translation by various hands was published in 1683, had no great opinion of either: 'That (sc. North's) translation was only from the French…it was a copy of a copy, and that too but lamely taken from the Greek original…(it) is not only ungrammatical and ungraceful, but in many places almost unintelligible'. Dryden was paid in kind when John and William Langhorne published their translation in 1770. 'To translate Plutarch under any circumstances,' they wrote, 'would require no ordinary skill in the language and antiquities of Greece'; but 'That great man, whose name is never to be mentioned without pity and admiration, was prevailed upon...to head a company of translators.... The diversities of style were not the greatest fault of this strange translation. It was full of the grossest errors. Ignorance on the one hand, and hastiness or negligence on the other, had filled it with absurdities in every life, and inaccuracies in almost every page. The language, in general, was insupportably tame, tedious, and embarrassed. The periods had no harmony; the phraseology had no elegance, no spirit, no precision.' The Langhornes' own version, in the opinion of George Wyndham, a stout champion of North, is pre-eminent among 'the cold perversions of a later age'. A.H. Clough disparages it as 'so inferior in liveliness' (sc. to Dryden) '...so dull and heavy a book' that it justifies his revision of Dryden (1859-60).

In entering this austere company, where Barrow's comment on Clough – 'unremarkable (yet) serviceable' – surprises by its charity, I have thought it wise to aim low. I have not tried to capture the character of Plutarch's Greek, but to express clearly what he said, and my sentences are characteristically shorter and more direct than his. This translation is for the use of those who do not know Greek, but want to know what Plutarch wrote, and had I attempted to reproduce his style, the English would often have been an impediment. Even North's version of Galba 1.3-4, for instance, which breaks a single sentence of Plutarch in two, needs careful reading: 'Therefore Plato, that saith it litle prevaileth to have a good and wise Captaine, if the souldiers also be not wise and obedient, thinking it as requisite for the vertue of obedience, to have men of a noble minde and good education, as otherwise it is meete for a Captaine to know how to direct and commaunde well, considering it is that which with lenity and mildnes doth mitigate all fury and choller: he hath divers other examples and sufficient proofes to prove his words true, and namely, the great miseries and calamities which came to the Romanes after the death of Nero, do plainly shew, that nothing is more daungerous nor dreadfull in an Empire, then a great armie living licentiouslie and disorderly.'

Yet a style simpler than Plutarch's may have its own kind of propriety. His was not unmodish. It was a personal variant on the literary idiom of his day, and if that is a justification for representing it in the idiom of our time, the structures will be simple. Here the Renaissance translators had a great advantage over us in trying to meet Amyot's exacting standard: the Latinate structure of their language was intrinsically closer to Plutarch's than the unceremonial directness of ours. There is much in the sturdy vigour of North's turn of phrase that the modern translator must admire. Otho was 'ever geven to sensualitie and pleasure from his cradell' (*Galba* 19.1); Tigellinus lusted incorrigibly in 'following naughtie packes, and common strumpets, burning still in filthie concupiscence' (*Otho* 2.1); the soldiers dethroned Galba with a Shakespearian 'Hence, hence, privat man' (*Galba* 26.5). We cannot imitate such turns without making Plutarch appear quaint; and, however right North's elaborate Renaissance sentences are in one sense, we cannot imitate them either without making him appear archaic.

Notes to the Introduction

1. This depends on the reading and interpretation of Josephus, *Jew. Ant.* XIX 91-2.

2. The text translated is that of the Budé edition of F. Flacelière and É. Chambry (Paris, 1979).

3. From Sir Thomas North's translation of Amyot's 'Foreword', which North included in the preface to his translation of Amyot.

4. Ibid.

5. Ibid.

6. Ziegler 937.

7. '*Im ganzen* (bleiben die langen Perioden P.s) *meist* durchsichtig, wenn sie auch...einen merksamen Leser verlangen' (ibid. 938, my emphasis – D.L.).

8. The juxtaposition of vowels at the end of one word and the beginning of the next. For avoidance of hiatus in English, compare the use of 'an' for 'a' before vowels (as 'an egg').

The *Life* of Galba

1.1 The Athenian Iphicrates believed that a mercenary soldier should love wealth and pleasure: seeking the means to satisfy his desires he would fight more recklessly. Most, however, maintain that troops should never follow their own impulse, but be moved like a single body by the will of their commander. **2** Thus, so they say, when Aemilius Paulus took over the army in Macedonia, which was full of 'advisers' and other upstarts, as though it was its own High Command, he instructed it to keep its hands ready and its swords sharp – he would take care of the rest. **3** Plato saw that a good leader and a good general were useless if their army lacked self-discipline and a sense of unity. He believed that true obedience, like true kingship, demands nobility of nature and a philosophic upbringing, since this above all will blend passion of spirit and vigour of body harmoniously with gentleness and a concern for others. **4** As examples which prove his case that nothing is more terrible in an empire than military force governed by shortsighted and irrational impulses, one could cite many disasters, and pre-eminently those which fell upon Rome after the death of Nero. **5** When Alexander died, Demades, seeing the constant upheavals, disorder and confusion in the Macedonian army, compared it to the blinded Cyclops. **6** The Roman Empire fell victim to disasters and upheavals like those of the 'War of the Titans'. It tore itself to pieces which met again in a war fought from all quarters of the compass – not so much through a hunger for power in those proclaimed emperor as through indiscipline and hunger for money in the troops, who, as nail drives out nail, drove emperor out by emperor. **7** Dionysius, wittily alluding to the swiftness of the reversal, called Polyphron of Pherae the 'king of tragedy'; yet Polyphron, before his abrupt dispatch, ruled Thessaly for ten months. **8** In shorter space than that four emperors occupied the Palatine, the home of the Caesars. As if on a stage one was given his entry while the other was given his exit. **9** There was, however, one consolation for the suffering people. They needed no vengeance on the guilty beyond the sight of their being slaughtered by each other. First to fall, and most justly, was the one who had bribed Roman soldiers and taught them to expect all he himself promised as the price for slaying Caesars. By his fee for service he defiled a noble deed and made the revolt against Nero an act of betrayal.

2.1 Nymphidius Sabinus, as I have said, shared the command of the Praetorian Guard with Tigellinus. When Nero had abandoned all hope and was clearly planning escape to Egypt, Sabinus, alleging that the emperor was no longer at Rome but already in flight, persuaded his troops to proclaim Galba emperor. **2** He promised every soldier of the Guard (the 'Palace' and 'Praetorian' Guards, as they are called) 7,500 denarii, and 1,250 to the legions abroad. This was a sum no man could conceivably put together without inflicting on all humanity sufferings infinitely greater than those inflicted by Nero. **3** This promise finished Nero then and there, and Galba soon after: the military deserted one in hope of reward, and killed the other when the hope proved false. **4** Then, in search of a leader who would pay that colossal bounty, they destroyed themselves by mutiny and betrayal before they ever touched their coveted prize. **5** Now to give an accurate, detailed account of events is the task of the historian proper; but it would not be right for me either to pass over in silence the most notable deeds and disasters of the Caesars.

3.1 Sulpicius Galba is generally acknowledged as the wealthiest of all private citizens who occupied the palace of the Caesars. The house of the Servii endowed him with the prestige of high nobility; he himself set more store by his kinship with Catulus, who in his own day had been unrivalled in moral character and public esteem, although he chose to let others wield superior power. **2** He was also related to Livia, the consort of Caesar, and for this reason Livia enabled him to leave from the Palatine when he entered on his consulship. **3** He is also said to have commanded with distinction in Germany, and, as proconsul of Libya, to have earned an admiration accorded to few. **4** When he became emperor the modesty of his way of life, his thrift and restraint were denigrated as meanness – he had the outmoded reputation, to put it that way, of self-discipline and moderation. **5** Nero, who had not yet learned to fear citizens held in high regard, sent him to Spain as governor. He seemed to be intrinsically unambitious, and his advanced age was a further guarantee of discretion.

4.1 There bloodsucking procurators were plundering the provincials on Nero's behalf with ruthless savagery. Galba could give the victims no practical help, but by showing clearly that he too felt the pain and injustice inflicted on them, he somehow gave them hope and relief even when they were condemned and sold into slavery. **2** When satirical verses against Nero appeared and were being circulated and sung everywhere, he did not prohibit them, nor did he share the indignation of the procurators. This made him still more popular among the general population, **3** and he was already well established in his province, and had held his command for seven years, when Julius Vindex, governor of Gaul, rebelled against Nero. **4** It is said that, even before the outbreak of the revolt, a letter from Vindex had reached Galba. He did not trust it, but neither did he report or denounce it, unlike other provincial commanders, who sent to Nero letters written to them and, in so far as they could, nullified an enterprise in which they later took part – an admission that they had been traitors to themselves as much as to Vindex. 5 When Vindex openly declared war he wrote to Galba urging him to accept the leadership and offer himself to a powerful body in search of a head, meaning the provinces of Gaul, which, he said, had 100,000 men under arms and the resources to arm more than as many again. 6 Galba consulted his friends, some of whom advised him to hold his hand until he saw how Rome would react to the uprising in Gaul. 7 Titus Vinius, however, commander of his personal guard, said 'Galba, what kind of plan is that? Merely to ask whether we will keep faith with Nero means that we have broken it already. If Nero is your enemy, don't reject an alliance with Vindex. Otherwise, denounce him now and fight him because he wants Rome to have you as ruler rather than Nero as tyrant.'

5.1 After this meeting Galba announced in a written proclamation the date on which he would confer freedom individually on those slaves who requested it. But rumour and report had already got about, and a crowd assembled enthusiastic for the revolution. No sooner had he appeared on the tribunal than all of them, with one voice, hailed him emperor. 2 For the moment he refused to accept the title. However, having condemned Nero and expressed grief for the death of his most illustrious victims he promised he would devote his care to the good of his country, not as 'Caesar' or 'emperor', but as general of the Senate and People of Rome. 3 Vindex had calculated well when he called on Galba to assume the leadership. He was proved right by Nero himself, who, though affecting to despise Vindex and regard the rising in Gaul as nothing, having heard the news of Galba while he was taking lunch after his bath, upended the table. 4 Nonetheless, when the Senate declared Galba a public enemy, wishing to present a front of nonchalant humour to his friends, he said that he needed money, and the perfect excuse for getting it had landed in his lap: 5 he would loot the Gauls once they were brought to heel, and the property of Galba, who was now his open enemy, was on hand to be used or sold. 6 He did in fact order Galba's possessions to be sold; when Galba heard of it he announced the sale of Nero's assets in Spain and found no dearth of enthusiastic buyers.

6.1 Many were now defecting from Nero, and virtually all of them declaring for Galba. Only two acted independently – Clodius Macer in Africa, and, in Gaul, Verginius Rufus, commander of the army in Germany – and they from different motives. 2 Clodius, grasping and sadistic, had made a career of robbery and murder. He was obviously vacillating, incapable of either keeping his command or giving it up. 3 Verginius was at the head of Rome's most formidable legions. They repeatedly proclaimed him emperor and tried to force his assent. His response was that he would neither accept the rule of the empire himself nor stand by while it was given to anyone not chosen by the Senate. 4 From the start this disquieted Galba deeply. Next the armies of Verginius and Vindex, virtually dragging their commanders into the field against their will as if they were charioteers who couldn't hold their teams, committed them to a great battle. Twenty thousand Gauls died; Vindex killed himself on the corpses. When a report spread abroad that in view of Verginius' outstanding victory everyone wanted him to assume supreme power, and that if he refused they would acknowledge Nero once more, 5 Galba became extremely alarmed and wrote to Verginius urging him to join forces and save Rome's freedom and the empire. 6 Then, taking his friends with him, he withdrew to the Spanish town of Clunia where he spent his time regretting what he had done and longing for his old, accustomed uncomplicated way of life rather than doing what was needed.

7.1 By now it was summer. One evening, just before dusk, his freedman Icelus arrived from Rome, having covered the distance in seven days. 2 Hearing that Galba was resting and alone, he hurried to his bedroom, brushed the attendants aside, opened the door, went up to Galba and told him that when Nero was still alive but in hiding, first the army, then the Senate and people had proclaimed him 'emperor', and that Nero's death had been reported soon after. 3 He had not, he said, left Rome because he trusted this report; he had gone himself and seen Nero lying dead. 4 The news re-vitalized Galba, and a crowd imbued with his confidence gathered at his door. 5 Yet Icelus' speed was unbelievable. However, two days later Titus...one of the Praetorians, arrived, and not alone, and reported the decisions of the Senate in detail. 6 Titus was promoted to a post of honour; on Icelus Galba conferred the right to the gold ring, and, now known as Marcianus, he became the dominant force among the emperor's freedmen.

8.1 Meanwhile in Rome Nymphidius Sabinus usurped complete control, and not by stealth or degrees but by comprehensive action: Galba was, he said, senile, and at that age it would tax his strength to be carried to Rome in a litter (he was seventy-three years old). 2 He had long been popular with the troops in Rome, and now they looked to him alone – and thanks to the extravagant reward he had promised them, they regarded him as their benefactor, Galba as their debtor. 3 His first act was to order Tigellinus, joint-commander of the Praetorian Guard, to give up his sword. He arranged functions at which he banqueted former consuls and leading senators, though he still sent the invitations under the name of Galba. In the praetorian camp he orchestrated numerous 'spontaneous' demands for a delegation to Galba requesting that Nymphidius should be sole commander, and for life. **4** All that the Senate did to increase his status and power – they named him 'public benefactor', trotted in packs to his door every day, and asked him to propose all their decrees and ratify them – made him still more presumptuous, and before long he was not only hated by his sycophants, but feared also. **5** Now decrees were delivered to the emperor by public slaves acting under instruction from the consuls, who provided them with their sealed 'diplomas', as they are called (the local authorities, acknowledging these, maintain the speed of the couriers by fast changes of vehicle). Nymphidius was incensed when they sent these messengers without using either his seal or his soldiers, **6** and, it is said, gave serious thought to the consuls till they mollified his anger by excuses and apologies. As a gesture to the crowd he did not prevent them beating to death anyone they came across who was associated with Nero. **7** They killed Spiculus the gladiator in the forum by throwing him under statues of Nero as they were being dragged away; they spread-eagled the informer Aponius and drove cartloads of rock over him; and they tore a considerable number to pieces, some of them completely innocent. **8** Finally Mauricus, a man who deserved his high reputation, was moved to say in the Senate that he was afraid they would soon miss Nero.

9.1 As Nymphidius came closer to realizing his hopes he did not discourage a rumour that he was the son of Tiberius' successor, Gaius Caesar. **2** It seemed that when Gaius was still in his teens he had been intimate with Nymphidius' mother, a not unattractive woman who was the daughter of a seamstress by the emperor's freedman Callistus. **3** Apparently, however, her relations with Gaius had occurred after the birth of Nymphidius. Less flattering report made him the son of the gladiator Martianus, whose reputation had proved irresistible to Nymphidia, and physical resemblance made this the more probable connection. **4** Still, while admitting that Nymphidia was his mother, he claimed sole credit for the removal of Nero. Nor did he think it was adequate reward to enjoy wealth and honours and sleep with Nero's lover Sporus (Nymphidius had sent for him immediately and had him brought from the pyre while the corpse was still burning, used him as his wife and called him Poppaea): he was angling for supreme power. **5** He himself, with the covert support of men of senatorial rank and certain women, worked surreptitiously in Rome through his friends; one of these, Gellianus, he sent to Spain for an eye-witness report.

10.1 After the death of Nero the tide of events ran strong for Galba, although Verginius Rufus still caused him concern. His stance was uncertain; he commanded a large army of formidable fighters; and now that he had defeated Vindex and subdued the whole of Gaul – a major part of the empire, which had been in revolutionary upheaval – he might lend his ear to those who were offering him supreme power. **2** He had no equal in glory or reputation, since he seemed to have played the decisive part in freeing Rome not only from a harsh tyranny, but also from a Gallic war. **3** At that time, however, holding fast to his original principle, he reserved the choice of emperor to the Senate. **4** Even so, when Nero's death was certain, his troops tried once more to persuade him, and one of the tribunes in his tent, drawing his sword, told him to accept the empire or the steel. **5** Then, after Fabius Valens, one of his legionary commanders, had been the first to swear his troops for Galba, and a letter arrived from Rome announcing the decree of the Senate, with great difficulty he persuaded his troops to proclaim Galba emperor. **6** He accepted Hordeonius Flaccus, who had been sent by Galba to replace him, and, having handed over his command, went to meet Galba on his approach, and turned back with him. He was received with neither obvious resentment nor favour – **7** the first because Galba respected his personal qualities, the second because of Galba's friends, and especially Titus Vinius who was jealous of Verginius and determined to bring him down. (Yet unwittingly he was the instrument of Verginius' guardian spirit which was already releasing him from the wars and troubles endured by the other leaders to a life of calm and an old age of peace and quiet.)

11.1 The representatives of the Senate met Galba at the Gallic city of Narbonne, made their greetings, and pressed him to present himself without delay to his yearning people. **2** In meetings and discussions he showed himself amiable and unpretentious. For his formal dinners he had at his disposal a full array of the imperial table-service and attendants, selected from Nero's and sent to him by Nymphidius. Galba ignored them, and, using nothing but his own, won respect as a man of principle and true breeding. **3** Vinius, however, denigrated this restraint, which was that of a high-minded and unassuming citizen, as 'populism' or 'such *delicate* scruples about one's right to the best', and soon persuaded him to use Nero's wealth and organize his receptions with right royal extravagance. **4** In short, the old man gave the impression that he would gradually become the puppet of Vinius.

12.1 Vinius had a profound, in fact unparalleled craving for money; he was also prone to acts of vice with women. **2** When he was still a young man he served his first campaign under Calvisius Sabinus. Calvisius' wife was a slut; one night Vinius smuggled her into the camp disguised as a soldier and enjoyed her in the general's headquarters (*principia*, as the Romans call them). **3** Gaius Caesar gaoled him for this, but when Gaius died he was luckily set free. **4** While a dinner-guest of the emperor Claudius he stole a silver goblet. Claudius, having discovered the theft, invited him back to dinner on the following evening, and, when he came, instructed his slaves to put no silver within his reach, only earthenware. **5** Thanks to Claudius' forbearance this episode ended on a comic note and seemed to merit ridicule rather than indignation. But what he did for money when he had made Galba his puppet and himself the ultimate power became for some the cause, for others the occasion of tragic sufferings and cruel disasters.

13.1 Gellianus, whom Nymphidius had sent to Spain effectively to spy on Galba, had returned posthaste to Rome with the news that Cornelius Laco had been appointed commander of the Palace and of the Praetorian Guards; that all power lay in the hands of Vinius; and that he himself had never managed to get near Galba or meet him privately since everyone had regarded him with suspicion and had watched him carefully. Nymphidius, profoundly alarmed, **2** called the officers of the Praetorian Guard to a meeting and told them that, while Galba was personally a well-meaning and moderate old man, he had resigned his own judgement and was being manipulated by Vinius and Laco to no good end. **3** Before they insinuated themselves into the position of power which Tigellinus had held, a delegation should be sent from the camp to the emperor advising him that if he cut off only those two from among his friends his arrival at Rome would be anticipated and welcomed more enthusiastically by all. **4** The officers were unconvinced. In fact, the notion of instructing a man of Galba's age and authority as to whom he should or should not treat as friends, as if he were a boy tasting power for the first time, struck them as absolutely ludicrous. Nymphidius then tried another tack. He began sending Galba disquieting messages: the city was dangerously unsettled, and rife with intrigue; in Libya Clodius Macer was holding back shipments of grain; the German legions were restless, and he had heard the same about the forces in Syria and Judaea. **5** When Galba, sceptical of these reports, ignored him completely, he decided to strike first, even though Clodius Celsus of Antioch – his loyal friend, despite being a man of sense – tried to dissuade him by saying that he didn't believe there was a slum in Rome that would hail Nymphidius as Caesar. **6** However, there were many who ridiculed Galba, such as Mithridates of Pontus. He, sneering at Galba's wrinkles and bald head, said that now the Romans thought he was someone, but once they had set eyes on him he would seem a stain on the days he was called Caesar.

14.1 It was decided, therefore, that an escort would take Nymphidius to the barracks at midnight and proclaim him emperor. **2** The first tribune to intervene was Antonius Honoratus. At dusk he assembled the troops under his command and condemned them, and himself. In a short time they had changed their mind far too often, and not from rational calculation or choice of a better alternative but as if a demon were hounding them from betrayal to betrayal. **3** Initially they had had the excuse of Nero's crimes, but now they were betraying Galba, and what matricide did they hold against him?

had he murdered his wife? or what lyre-strumming or tragic acting of his had degraded them? **4** 'Not that it was even for this reason,' he said, 'that we brought ourselves to desert Nero, but believing Nymphidius' lie that he had deserted us first and run away to Egypt. **5** Are we going to sacrifice Galba on Nero's tomb and by making Nymphidia's bastard emperor destroy Livia's descendant as we destroyed Agrippina's son? or will we make him pay for his crimes, and Rome look on us as avengers of Nero and true and loyal bodyguards of Galba?' **6** The tribune's speech persuaded his troops to a man. They then went around the others urging them to stand by their pledge to the emperor, and won most of them over. **7** A shout went up, and Nymphidius, believing, as some say, that the troops were already calling for him, or anxious to act first while the camp was still confused and divided, marched towards it under the light of numerous torches. In his hand was a papyrus roll containing a speech written by Cingonius Varro which he had rehearsed for delivery to the troops. **8** When he saw that the gates were shut and the walls lined with armed men his spirit sank, but he walked towards them and asked them what they were doing and who had given them the order to arm. **9** All replied in a single roar, 'Our emperor is Galba.' Taking up their cry, and telling his escort to do the same, he went up to the wall. **10** The guards on the gates admitted him and a few others. Someone threw a javelin at him which Septimius, walking ahead of him, took on his shield. He broke away, but they followed him and dispatched him in a soldier's bedroom. **11** Then, having dragged the corpse into the middle of the camp and fenced it off, they entertained the curious with the spectacle the following day.

15.1 That was the end of Nymphidius. When Galba heard of it, he ordered the conspirators who had not been killed with him on the spot to be put to death, among them Cingonius, who had written the speech, and Mithridates of Pontus. However just, this execution without trial of men of high standing was felt to be neither lawful nor humane. **2** This was not the kind of government the people had expected, deceived, as usual, by fine promises at the outset. They were offended still more by the forced suicide of Petronius Turpilianus, an ex-consul who had remained loyal to Nero. **3** When Galba had Macer killed in Libya by Trebonius and Fonteius in Germany by Valens he could at least claim they were a threat, since both men were on active service with their armies. **4** But why should an emperor who intended to practice the moderation he professed in his letters have refused a hearing to Turpilianus, a defenceless and unarmed old man? **5** Such was the criticism which these acts incurred. Then when he himself, on his approach to Rome, was about five kilometres from the city, he encountered a wild demonstration by oarsmen who blocked the road and hemmed him in on all sides. **6** These were the ones whom Nero had organized into one legion and designated 'soldiers', and they were there to make sure their military status was confirmed. They prevented those who had come to meet the emperor from being seen or heard, but with riotous bawling demanded standards and quarters for their legion. 7 Galba tried to put them off and told them to speak to him later, but they claimed the delay was tantamount to a refusal, and their mood turned ugly. They kept pace beside him shouting uproariously until, when some of them even drew their swords, Galba ordered his cavalry to charge. 8 None of them resisted; some were cut down on the spot, others slaughtered as they ran, creating a grim and sinister omen for Galba, who entered the city through a mess of blood and corpses. 9 Before, there had been those who despised him as a feeble old man; now all looked on him with fear and apprehension.

16.1 Intending, again, to reverse Nero's reckless extravagance in handing out gifts, he seemed to go too far. 2 The flute-player Canus, a renowned musician, was once performing for him during dinner. Galba applauded him, received him at his table, and ordered his cash-box to be brought. Then he took a few gold coins and gave them to Canus, saying that it was his money he was giving, not the state's. 3 He gave strict instructions that nine-tenths of the value of the gifts Nero had made to actors and athletes should be demanded back. Since the proceeds were negligible (these people are satyrs and live for the day, and most of them had squandered everything) he set about finding those to whom they had sold or given anything, and claimed restitution from them. 4 But there was no end to the process – the net spread wide and entangled many – and Galba himself became unpopular, and Vinius envied and abhorred: while making the emperor a mean-minded accountant, he himself was taking everything, selling everything, and squandering millions. 5 According to Hesiod we should

Drink up when the jar is near full, or near done....

Vinius, seeing that Galba was old and frail, gorged himself on the gifts of Fortune as if, when she first came, she was already slipping away.

17.1 The old man was not only the scapegoat for Vinius' abuse of power – the sensible decisions Galba made himself Vinius either thwarted or misrepresented. 2 The punishment of Nero's associates was a case in point. Galba executed the worst, among others Helius, Polycleitus, Petinus and Patrobius. 3 The people acclaimed their condemnation, and when they were being paraded through the forum shouted that this was a procession beautiful to look upon and applauded in heaven, but they called on gods and men to give them the architect and overseer of the tyranny, Tigellinus. This noble Roman had, however, covered his tracks by generous retainers to

Vinius; **4** thus Turpilianus, who was hated for not hating and betraying an emperor such as Nero (this was the sole serious charge against him) was dead, but the man who made Nero deserve to die then abandoned the monster he had created was unscathed – conspicuous proof that nothing was impossible for Vinius, nor beyond hope for those who could pay him. **5** There was no spectacle the Romans craved more dearly than the sight of Tigellinus on his way to execution and in every theatre and every stadium they never stopped calling for his blood. They were reprimanded in an edict from the emperor declaring that Tigellinus was suffering from a terminal illness and did not have long to live, and requesting them not to make the administration ruthless and tyrannical. **6** The people were enraged, but Tigellinus and Vinius derided them openly, Tigellinus by a thanksgiving sacrifice for release from peril and staging a lavish banquet, Vinius by rising after a dinner with the emperor and going to Tigellinus' house in a celebratory procession, taking his widowed daughter with him. Tigellinus, having toasted her with a pledge of one million sesterces, told his number one concubine to take off her necklace and put it on the widow. It was said to be worth 600,000 sesterces.

18.1 From this time a hostile construction was put even on Galba's reasonable actions, such as those in regard to the Gauls who had rebelled with Vindex – **2** they were felt to owe their remission of tribute and right of citizenship not to any generosity of the emperor but to a cash deal with Vinius. **3** For these reasons the general public began to resent Galba's rule; the troops, on the other hand, although they had not received their promised donative, were deluded in the beginning by the hope that even if he did not give the full amount he would at least give as much as Nero. **4** When he heard of their complaints, however, and responded with an utterance worthy of a great leader – 'I am accustomed to enlist my troops, not buy them' – they, once aware of it, conceived a bitter and savage hatred for him: **5** he was not only swindling them himself, he was establishing a precedent for future emperors as well. **6** At Rome the unrest was still beneath the surface; Galba's presence inspired respect and checked and blunted the impulse to mutiny, and because the troops could see no clear sign that a revolution had begun they more or less repressed and concealed their hostility. **7** But the legions which had previously been under Verginius and were now under Flaccus in Germany believed they deserved generous reward for their battle against Vindex, and when they received nothing began to defy their commanders. **8** They paid no regard whatsoever to Flaccus himself who was naïve in practical matters and physically incapacitated by severe gout; **9** and once, when a show was being put on and the tribunes and centurions were reciting a prayer (as is customary among the Romans) for 'good fortune for the emperor Galba', most of the soldiers greeted it with catcalls, and when the officers persisted with their prayer, added 'If he deserves it!'

19.1 As the legions under Vitellius also frequently committed similar acts of insolence, letters were sent to Galba from his procurators, and he, worried that he lacked authority not only because he was old but also because he was childless, decided to adopt a young man of high social standing, and name him his successor. **2** Now Marcus Otho was a man not undistinguished by birth, but hedonistic self-indulgence had corrupted him from childhood to a degree few Romans have equalled; and just as Homer often calls Paris 'the husband of Helen of the beautiful hair', glorifying through his wife a man who had no other claim to renown, so Otho had become famous at Rome for his marriage to Poppaea. **3** Nero had been infatuated with her when she was married to Crispinus, but as he still had some respect for his own wife and was afraid of his mother, he employed Otho to try her virtue. **4** Otho, thanks to his profligacy, was already a friend and boon-companion of Nero, who was vastly diverted by his regular taunts of stinginess and penny-pinching. **5** The story is told that when Nero was being anointed with a priceless unguent he poured it all over Otho. On the following day Otho entertained him in turn, and suddenly opened gold and silver pipes from all directions simultaneously which poured out myrrh like water and left the guests doused. **6** Having debauched Poppaea on Nero's behalf, then seduced her further by holding out hopes of the emperor himself, he persuaded her to leave her husband. **7** When she came to Otho as a bride, however, he was reluctant to share her favours and deplored the *ménage à trois*; nor was Poppaea herself, so they say, displeased at his jealousy. **8** Indeed, it is said that once while Otho was away she shut the door on Nero, either to avoid cloying him with pleasure, or, as some allege, feeling that marriage to Caesar would be an inconvenience, but not being averse, due to her penchant for stolen fruits, to enjoying him as a lover. **9** In consequence Otho was in danger of his life, and it is paradoxical that he should have been spared by the emperor who murdered his own wife and sister to marry Poppaea.

20.1 He did, however, have the support of Seneca, and as a result of his persuasive advice to Nero Otho was sent to the Atlantic coast as praetor of Lusitania. **2** Here he showed himself neither unamiable nor oppressive to those he governed, well aware that the position he had been given was exile under a sweeter-sounding name. **3** When Galba defected he was the first in a post of authority to join him, and taking all the silver and gold tables and drinking-vessels he had he gave them to him to melt down for the coinage Galba was minting. He also made him a present of those among his slaves who were practised in discreet attention to the day to day needs of a member of the élite. **4** In other respects, too, he was a loyal follower, and proved by his actions that in practical competence he was second to none. Throughout Galba's whole journey he rode with him continuously for days on end in the same carriage. 5 In the intimacy afforded by shared travel he ingratiated himself with Vinius by seeking his company and giving him gifts. Above all, by yielding Vinius the first place he won the favour which secured the second for himself. Yet even so he was superior: no one hated him, as he did for nothing whatever he was asked, and showed himself friendly and approachable to all. 6 He was particularly obliging to the soldiers and had many promoted to commands which he sometimes requested from Galba and sometimes cajoled from Vinius and the freedmen Icelus and Asiaticus; these were the most powerful of the circle about the emperor. 7 Whenever he entertained Galba he bought popularity with the cohort on guard by handing out a gold piece all round – ostensibly honouring the emperor, but in fact making a calculated bid for the goodwill of the troops.

21.1 Accordingly, when Galba was pondering on the succession, Vinius suggested Otho – as usual, not without a price, which in this case was the marriage of his daughter. The two had struck a deal that Otho would marry her after he had been proclaimed Galba's son and successor. 2 Galba consistently made it clear, however, that he put the public interest before his own, and that he was bent on adopting not the man who was most attractive to him, but most beneficial to Rome. 3 In all likelihood he would not have made Otho sole heir even to his personal estate, knowing that he was wasteful and licentious and immersed in debts of 200 million sesterces. Having therefore heard Vinius out politely and without interruption, he postponed his decision. 4 He then appointed himself consul with Vinius as his colleague, and it was expected that he would announce his successor at the beginning of the coming year. The preference of the military was unequivocally for Otho.

22.1 He was still vacillating and weighing options when the mutiny in Germany burst upon him. 2 The soldiers, everywhere and without exception, hated him for not having paid their donative, but the German legions had two particular grievances: one, that the removal of Verginius had been an insult to him; the other, that the Gauls who had fought against them were being rewarded, while those who had not joined Vindex were being victimized – Galba was grateful to him alone, honouring him in death and making state sacrifices to his spirit in the belief that it was due to him that he had been proclaimed emperor of Rome. 3 By New Year's Day (which the Romans call the Kalends of January) resentments such as these were being expressed openly throughout the camp, 4 and when Flaccus assembled the troops to swear the traditional oath of loyalty to the emperor they made for Galba's statues and tipped them over and pulled them down. Then, after swearing an oath to the Senate and People of Rome, they dispersed. **5** The officers were struck with apprehension that that this was not mere insubordination, but revolution, and at a meeting one of them said **6** 'Comrades, what has got into us? We are neither defending the present emperor nor choosing a new one, as though it is not Galba we are against but the very idea of submission to authority. **7** Forget about Hordeonius Flaccus – he is nothing more than a shadow of a shadow of Galba – but one day's march from here is Vitellius, governor of the other half of Germany. His father was censor and three times consul, and, in a sense, joint ruler with Claudius Caesar, and his own poverty, although some may sneer at it, is shining proof of personal integrity and greatness of soul. **8** So make up your minds! Choose Vitellius, and show the world that we are better judges of emperors than Spaniards or Portuguese.' **9** Some accepted his proposal outright, others opposed it, but a standard-bearer slipped alone out of the camp and took the news to Vitellius, who received it by night while entertaining a large company. **10** Word spread through the army and on the following day Fabius Valens, who was in command of one legion, rode up with a strong force of cavalry, and saluted Vitellius as emperor – the first to do so. **11** Throughout the previous days Vitellius had seemed to be rejecting the prospect, or rather shrinking from it, intimidated by the huge responsibility. However, at this moment, so they say, he was full of wine and mid-day food and listened complaisantly while they hailed him 'Germanicus', although he refused the title of 'Caesar'. **12** Immediately the forces with Flaccus, forgetting their fine oaths of loyalty to the Senate, swore they would do what the emperor Vitellius commanded.

23.1 This is how Vitellius was proclaimed emperor in Germany. Once Galba heard of the revolt he deferred the adoption no longer. **2** He knew that some of his friends favoured Dolabella, but most of them Otho, although he himself approved of neither. Abruptly, without a word to anyone, he sent for Piso, the son of Nero's victims Crassus and Scribonia – a young man whose natural disposition to every kind of virtue was marked above all by austerity and a sense of propriety – and went out to the praetorian camp to proclaim him Caesar and his successor. **3** From the moment he set foot out of doors he was dogged by unmistakable portents, and as he began his speech in the camp (which he part read, part improvised) thunder roared and lightning flashed so often, and such darkness and torrents of rain enveloped the camp and the city, that it was patently obvious that the gods had set their face against the adoption, and that it would come to no good. **4** The soldiers too were sullen and resentful since even now he offered them no donative. **5** In spite of that Piso won the admiration of those who were present: they could tell by his voice and his expression that he accepted this honour of honours with composure, yet not without emotion. Similarly many signs in Otho's demeanour betrayed the burning fury with which he endured the disappointment of a hope which had been held out to him first and which he had been within an ace of realizing. The rebuff was, he assumed, an indication of hostility and disaffection towards him on the part of Galba. **6** He was, therefore, more than a little uneasy about the future, and left the camp fearing Piso, accusing Galba, and cursing Vinius, in short, full of diverse sensations, **7** since he could not abandon his hopes or give up altogether. The Chaldaeans who were always hanging round him prevented that, and especially Ptolemaeus, whose opinion carried weight after his repeated predictions that Otho would not die at the hands of Nero, who would die first himself, but survive to become ruler of Rome. Having proved the first prediction true, he urged Otho not to despair of the second either. **8** He was encouraged not least by secret sympathizers, and those who felt for him as the victim of ingratitude. Most of those who had enjoyed status as friends of Tigellinus and Nymphidius and were now cast aside and living the life of the humbled joined him with enthusiasm, shared his resentment, and spurred him on.

24.1 Among these were Veturius and Barbius, the first an *optio*, the second a *tesserarius* (these titles are given to men serving as messengers or observers). **2** By dint of repeated approaches these two, with Otho's freedman Onomastus, corrupted some of the Praetorians with cash, others with handsome prospects. Obviously they were already undeclared traitors waiting only for an excuse – **3** to change the allegiance of a loyal corps was not the work of the four days which separated the adoption from the murders, and it was on the sixth day (the eighteenth before the Kalends of February by the Roman reckoning) that they were killed. **4** At dawn on that day Galba was sacrificing on the Palatine in the company of friends. As soon as the priest Umbricius took the victim's entrails in his hand he said – and not in riddles but in plain words – that he saw the portents of a great upheaval, and danger hatched by treason hanging over the emperor's head. The god was virtually handing Otho over to arrest: **5** he was there, behind Galba, listening intently to Umbricius as he interpreted and explained the signs. **6** As he stood aghast, his cheeks now burning, now white with fear, his freedman Onomastus went up to him and said that the builders had come and were waiting for him at home. This was the signal for the moment at which Otho was to join the soldiers. **7** Saying, therefore, that he had bought an old house and wanted to point out apparent defects to the vendors, he left the sacrifice, and going through the so-called 'house of Tiberius' reached the forum at the point where the golden pillar stands which marks the end of all the formed roads of Italy.

25.1 Authorities state that the first who met him there and hailed him emperor were twenty-three at the most; 2 and although Otho was not as effete in spirit as he was effeminate in body, but daring and resolute in the face of danger, his nerve failed. 3 The conspirators left him no choice. They drew their swords, surrounded his litter, and ordered the bearers to pick it up, with Otho moaning that he was done for and telling the bearers to run faster (a few bystanders heard the words, less in terror than astonishment at the hardihood of such a small band). 4 As he was being carried through the forum an equal number came to meet him. Then in threes and fours others joined in, and all of them turned back, saluting him as Caesar and holding out their drawn swords. 5 The tribune Martialis, officer of the guard at the camp, was reputedly ignorant of the plot, but he was taken aback and intimidated by their startling arrival and let Otho pass. 6 Once he was in there was no resistance. Those who did not know what was afoot found themselves encircled by a pre-concerted ring of those who did, and, at first in fear and in scattered ones and twos, and finally by assent, they joined the mutineers. 7 The news reached Galba on the Palatine immediately, while the priest was still there and still holding the entrails in his hands – a circumstance which provoked stupefaction and admiration of the divine power in even the most hardened sceptics. 8 As a motley mob poured up from the forum Vinius, Laco and a few of the imperial freedmen stood close to Galba holding out their drawn swords; Piso went to appeal to the palace guards; and the incorruptible Marius Celsus was sent to secure the loyalty of the Illyrian detachment which was quartered in the so-called 'portico of Vipsanius'.

26.1 While Galba, opposed by Vinius but encouraged by Celsus and Laco (both of whom made a cutting attack on Vinius), was debating whether to go forward, a persistent rumour spread that Otho had been killed in the camp. 2 Soon afterwards Julius Atticus, a well-known praetorian guard, appeared, running with his sword drawn and shouting that he had killed the enemy of Caesar. Forcing his way through the crowd he showed Galba the blade wet with blood. 3 Galba looked at him and said 'Who gave you the order?' The soldier replied 'Loyalty, and the oath I swore.' The crowd burst into applause and shouted 'Well said!', and Galba got into his litter and was carried away, intending to sacrifice to Jupiter and show himself to the citizens. 4 As he was hurried into the forum, like a breeze that had changed quarter the report greeted him that Otho was master of the praetorian camp. 5 While the crowd was roaring the advice typical of such a mob – to go on, to go back, to face it out, to distrust the report – and his litter, as if tossed by breakers, was being pulled backwards and forwards and often tipped on its side, first cavalry appeared, then soldiers on foot, charging through the basilica of Paulus and shouting as one man for the 'ex-emperor' to 'get out of the way'. 6 The crowd ran to the basilicas and vantage-points of the forum, scattering not in flight but as if they were finding seats for a show. **7** Atilius Vergilio hurled an effigy of Galba to the ground. That was the signal for war: encircling the litter they pelted it with javelins and when none of them hit Galba they rushed it with unsheathed swords. **8** No one defended him or resisted apart from a single man, the only one among all those thousands the sun looked on that day who was worthy of the Roman empire. His name was Sempronius Densus, and he was a centurion who had enjoyed no particular favour from Galba, but honouring right and law he stayed in front of the litter. **9** At first, raising the vine-wood staff with which the centurions thrash those who have incurred corporal punishment, in a loud voice he ordered the attackers to keep their hands off the emperor. **10** Then when they closed in on him he drew his sword and held them off for a long time until he was felled by a blow behind the knees.

27.1 Beside the Lacus Curtius, as it is called, Galba's litter was tipped over and he was thrown out. He was wearing a breastplate and they ran up and began hacking at him but he stretched out his neck and said 'Do it, if that is best for the Roman people.' **2** He received many wounds in the arms and legs; according to most accounts it was a certain Camurius of the fifteenth legion who killed him. **3** Some say, however, that it was Terentius, others Lecanius, and others Fabius Fabullus, who, they claim, cut off his head and, as it was bald and hard to hold, carried it away in his mantle. When those who were with him told him not to hide it, but to make his heroic act clear to the world, he impaled it on a spear – this head of an old man who had been high priest and consul and a conscientious ruler – and ran brandishing it like a bacchante, whirling around and around and shaking the spear as it dripped with blood. **5** Sources assert that when the head was brought to Otho he exclaimed 'But this is nothing, comrades! Show me Piso's head!' **6** It was brought before long. The young man had been wounded, and pursued when he tried to get away, then killed by a certain Murcus near the temple of Vesta. **7** Vinius was killed also despite his tacit admission that he had joined the conspiracy against Galba: he kept shouting that they were murdering him against the wishes of Otho. **8** It made no difference. They cut off his head too, and Laco's, and, taking them to Otho, demanded a reward. **9** Archilochus wrote:

> We caught up with seven and downed them as they ran –
> now seven hundred heroes claim each man.

It was the same then: many who took no part in the killing flaunted hands and swords they had smeared with blood themselves and handed Otho written appeals for reward. **10** It is a fact, at least, that one hundred and twenty were identified from their petitions; Vitellius hunted them down and killed the lot. **11** Marius Celsus also went to the camp. Many acccused him of having tried to persuade the troops to defend Galba, and the crowd roared for his death, but Otho was against it. **12** Being afraid to contradict them, he said they should not kill him so hastily, as there was certain information to be extracted from him first. He therefore told them to tie him up and keep him under guard, and handed him over to the troops he could rely on most.

28.1 The Senate was called immediately, and, as though they were different senators or were swearing by different gods, they assembled and took the oath of loyalty to Otho which he himself had taken and betrayed; and they proclaimed him Caesar and Augustus while the headless corpses were still lying in the forum in their consular robes. **2** When the killers had no more use for the heads they sold Vinius' to his daughter for 10,000 sesterces, released Piso's to his wife Verania after she had asked for it, and presented Galba's to the slaves of Patrobius. **3** Once they had their hands on it they subjected it to every kind of vile indignity then dumped it at the spot (it is called 'Sessorium') where those condemned by the Caesars are executed. **4** With Otho's permission Helvidius Priscus removed Galba's body, and the freedman Argius buried it after dark.

29.1 Such was the fate of Galba, a man second to few Romans in birth and wealth, and, by his wealth and birth, pre-eminent among all his contemporaries. **2** He lived under the rule of five emperors with honour and respect, and having overthrown Nero more by virtue of this respect than by military force.... Some of those who rebelled with him at the time no one thought worthy of supreme power, others judged themselves unworthy. **3** Galba, hailed emperor, accepted the title, and lending his name to Vindex' daring initiative turned a revolutionary disturbance, as his rebellion was called, into a civil war by giving it a true leader. **4** Believing therefore that he was not so much usurping control of the empire as giving himself to its service, he thought he could rule a people corrupted by Tigellinus and Nymphidius as Scipio, Camillus and Fabricius had ruled the Romans of old. **5** Even undermined by old age he was, in the sphere of practical military command, an emperor of sterling traditional qualities; but as Nero had made himself the pawn of his most insatiable favourites he made himself the pawn of Vinius, Laco and his freedmen, who turned government into a cash transaction, and left no one regretting his rule, but most pitying his death.

The *Life* of Otho

1.1 The new emperor went to the Capitol at dawn and made sacrifice; and having ordered Marius Ceslus to be brought before him greeted him warmly and spoke to him graciously, telling him to forget he had ever been accused rather than remember that he had been set free.   **2** Celsus' reply lacked neither dignity nor tact. The accusation was, he said, a proof of his moral character, since he had been accused of loyalty to Galba, a man to whom he owed no personal obligation. The bystanders were impressed by both men, and the troops applauded their 'reconciliation'.   **3** In the Senate Otho spoke at length in winning and generous style. He conferred on Verginius Rufus part of the time for which he was due to be consul himself, and confirmed all the appointments to the consulship made by Nero and Galba.   **4** He honoured with priesthoods men of advanced age or high reputation, and he restored to all of senatorial rank who had been exiled by Nero and recalled by Galba as much of their property as he could find still unsold.   **5** Previously, Romans of rank and influence had lived in terror, as if no man but an avenging Fury or bloodthirsty demon had suddenly fallen on the state, but now their hopes rose and they looked more kindly on a government which showed this smiling face.

2.1 Yet nothing delighted the whole population nor won their hearts for Otho more than his treatment of Tigellinus.   **2** He was already suffering unseen torment from the very fear of the punishment which the city demanded as a public debt, and from incurable physical diseases; while right-thinking men regarded his filthy, unspeakable bedsports with whores and vile women (which his incorrigible lust still hungered for and clutched after as he died by slow degrees) as the ultimate retribution and worse than a thousand deaths.   **3** Nonetheless it was generally considered an outrage that he was still looking on the light of day after he had quenched it for so many noble Romans, and Otho sent for him. He was living on his estate near Sinuessa, with boats moored close by in readiness for further flight.   **4** At first he offered the messenger a huge bribe to let him go, and, when he refused, gave him gifts even so, and asked him to wait until he had a shave. The messenger consented, and Tigellinus cut his own throat.

3.1 The emperor, having given the people this well-justified gratification, showed no trace of malice towards his personal enemies. Initially, however, out of deference to the crowd, he did not object to being addressed as Nero in the theatres, and did not prevent certain individuals from publicly displaying statues of Nero. **2** Cluvius Rufus writes that the letters of authority (those given couriers for their journeys) were taken to Spain bearing Nero's name added to that of Otho. However, Otho realized that Romans of rank and influence resented the practice, and gave it up. **3** While the stability of his rule was being established along these lines, the mercenaries began to cause trouble. They urged him not to trust the social élite but to be on his guard against them and check their power – either because they wished him well and were genuinely worried, or were using this pretext to manufacture disorder and conflict. **4** When Crispinus, whom he had sent to transfer the seventeenth cohort from Ostia, began to pack the equipment and load the weapons onto carts while it was still dark, the most insubordinate joined in rowdy accusations that he had not come for any decent purpose but that the Senate was staging a coup and the weapons were being taken to destroy Caesar, not protect him. **5** This fiction excited and outraged many. Some of them laid hold of the carts; the two centurions and Crispinus himself, who tried to stop them, were killed by others. Then all of them armed, and, calling on one another to rescue Caesar, marched to Rome. **6** There, hearing that he was entertaining eighty men of senatorial rank at dinner, they made for the palace, saying that now was the chance to annihilate Caesar's enemies at a stroke. **7** Panic seized the population, who expected the city to be sacked out of hand. In the palace there was a frantic to and fro, and Otho was confronted with a delicate problem. **8** While he feared for his guests, they feared him, and he saw their eyes fixed on him in wordless terror (some of them had brought their wives to the dinner also). **9** He sent the commanders of the Praetorian Guard to speak to the soldiers and calm them down; at the same time he told the guests to rise from table, and let them out through another door. **10** They escaped only seconds before the mercenaries forced their way into the dining-room demanding to know where the enemies of Caesar had got to. **11** For the moment, and with difficulty, he persuaded them to leave by standing on his couch and making repeated pleas and appeals, not even refraining from tears. **12** The next day, having presented every man with 1,250 denarii, he went to the camp. There he praised the majority for their zeal and devotion, but declared there were a few who, with sinister intent, were surreptitiously discrediting his moderation and the guards' loyalty, and asked them to join him in condemning and punishing their folly. **13** There was general applause and approval, but having arrested only two whose punishment was unlikely to offend anyone, he left the camp.

4.1 Those who already admired and trusted Otho applauded these acts as proof of reformation; others regarded them as ploys which the situation forced on a man seeking popular support in the face of war. **2** There were in fact already reliable reports that Vitellius had assumed the rank and authority of emperor. Couriers were constantly arriving with news of repeated defections in his favour, although others announced that the armies of Pannonia, Dalmatia and Moesia and their commanders had taken sides for Otho. **3** Before long letters of support came in from Mucianus and Vespasian, both of whom were at the head of powerful forces, one in Syria, the other in Judaea. **4** Encouraged by these he wrote to Vitellius urging him to consider an agreement under which Otho would provide him with a handsome sum of money and a city in which he could live undisturbed and in perfect ease and pleasure. Vitellius' initial response was peaceable, if ironic, **5** but later, as their bitterness grew, they wrote taunting each other with insults and foul abuse – with all truth, admittedly, yet it was a ludicrous absurdity that one should damn the other for vices that afflicted them both. **6** At least, it would be difficult to say which of them was the more profligate, effeminate, ignorant of warfare and ridden with debt incurred in the days before their affluence. **7** Many portents and apparitions were reported, most of them the product of vague anonymous rumours. **8** Everybody noticed, however, that the reins had fallen from the hands of a Victory mounted on her chariot on the Capitol as though she could not control them, and that the statue of Gaius Caesar on the island in the Tiber turned from west to east although there had been neither wind nor earthquake. **9** This allegedly happened about the time at which Vespasian began openly to take a hand in affairs. **10** Most also regarded the calamitous flooding of the Tiber as a baleful sign. It was the season at which rivers generally run full, but it had never risen so high before, nor wrought such comprehensive destruction – it burst its banks and inundated a large part of the city, especially that where they sell the grain available for purchase, and a distressing shortage of several days ensued.

5.1 At Rome, when it was reported that Vitellius' generals Caecina and Valens already controlled the Alps, Dolabella, a man of patrician family, roused a suspicion among the Praetorian Guards that he was plotting revolution. Otho, afraid either of him, or of others because of him, sent him to the town of Aquinum with expressions of reassurance. **2** Among the magistrates he selected for his campaign staff he included Vitellius' brother Lucius, neither increasing nor detracting from his honours. **3** He also took scrupulous care to allay any fears which Vitellius' wife and mother might have for their safety. **4** He appointed Vespasian's brother Flavius Sabinus Prefect of Rome, this too, perhaps, in honour of Nero (Galba had removed him from the post which had been conferred on him by Nero), or by promoting Sabinus he may rather have been demonstrating his goodwill towards and confidence in Vespasian. **5** He himself, then, stayed at Brixellum, an Italian town on the Po, and as commanders of his forces sent out Marius Celsus and Suetonius Paulinus, as well as Gallus and Spurinna. These were men who had made their mark, but on this campaign their calculations and decisions were thwarted by the insolence and insubordination of their troops: **6** as their hands had bestowed his authority on the emperor they thought it beneath them to listen to others. **7** On the enemy side too discipline was rather less than sound – the trooops were not amenable to orders but self-willed and arrogant for the same reason. **8** Yet they at least had experience of war, and being used to hardship were willing to endure it; Otho's troops, on the other hand, were soft from leisure and a life of peace in which they had devoted most of their time to the theatre and public shows and festivals, but they wanted to hide their softness behind bragging and insubordination and scorned routine duties as though they found them demeaning rather than too demanding. **9** When Spurinna tried to force them they came very close to killing him, and spared him no insult or abuse, calling him a traitor and a saboteur of Caesar's interests and opportunities. **10** Some of them even came to his tent at night drunk and demanded a travel-allowance – they were obliged, they said, to go to Caesar to lay charges against him.

6.1 Spurinna's situation was improved temporarily by the derision heaped on his army at Piacenza. **2** When Vitellius' forces attacked the walls they jeered at Otho's troops who were in position on the ramparts, calling them actors and ballet-dancers and expert spectators at Pythian and Olympic games but pure novices in war, since they'd never watched that, and too big for their boots after cutting off the head of a defenceless old soldier (meaning Galba) but refusing the challenge of a straightout fight with men. **3** They were so shaken and incensed by these insults that they fell on their knees before Spurinna and begged him to give them his orders and put them to work – they would accept every hardship and danger. **4** In a fierce battle for the wall in which the attackers brought many heavy siege-weapons into play Spurinna's troops won the day, and having driven the enemy off with heavy losses held an illustrious city which was one of the most flourishing in Italy. **5** Otho's generals were, moreover, less trying for both cities and individuals to deal with than those of Vitellius. **6** Caecina, engaging in neither language nor demeanour, was outlandish and nasty. A giant of a man, he addressed citizen assemblies and Roman magistrates alike wearing Gallic trousers and full-length sleeves. Picked cavalrymen escorted his wife, who rode on horseback decked out like a queen. **7** Vitellius' other general was Fabius Valens. Neither plunder from enemies nor loot and bribes from allies could satisfy his hunger for money, and it was through this that he was thought to have delayed his advance and arrived too late for the first battle. **8** Some, however, assert that Caecina, in his eagerness to claim the victory before Valens could join him, committed other less critical blunders, and fought the battle at the wrong time and for an unworthy motive, all but ruining their entire campaign.

7.1 After his repulse at Piacenza Caecina started for Cremona, which is also a large and prosperous city. Annius Gallus, while marching to Piacenza in support of Spurinna, heard that the defenders of Piacenza had been victorious, but that Cremona was in danger. He was the first to divert his army there, where he pitched camp close to the enemy; subsequently the other generals joined him in support. **2** In terrain covered in forest and underbrush Caecina posted a strong legionary force in ambush. He then ordered his cavalry to ride forward and, if the enemy engaged them, to withdraw gradually as if in retreat and so lure them into the ambush. Deserters, however, reported this to Celsus **3** who rode out against them with a tried band of cavalry, pursued them watchfully, surrounded and broke up the ambush, then summoned his infantry from the camp. **4** Had they arrived in time they would probably not have left one of the enemy alive but shattered and annihilated Caecina's whole army in the wake of the cavalry. As it was, Paulinus, who first delayed, then advanced too slowly in support, was condemned for over-caution and leadership unworthy of his reputation. **5** Most of the soldiers accused him of outright treachery and tried to turn Otho against him, boasting that they had won the battle and that the victory would have been final but for the cowardice of their commanders. **6** Otho did not so much believe them as he wished to avoid the appearance of not believing them. He therefore posted his brother Titianus to the army and Proculus, commander of the Praetorian Guard, who in fact had all the power, Titianus being a mere figurehead. **7** Celsus and Paulinus assumed the empty titles of 'counsellors' and 'friends'; in practice their influence and authority were nil. **8** There was unrest among the enemy also, and especially those under Valens' command. When they heard of the battle around the ambush they were indignant that they had not been there to fight when so many men had been killed. **9** They were determined to stone him, but grudgingly gave way to his entreaties, and Valens broke camp and joined forces with Caecina.

8.1 When Otho arrived at the camp at Bedriacum (a small town near Cremona) he weighed the arguments for and against battle. **2** Proculus and Titianus, pointing to the enthusiasm of the troops and their recent victory, said he should fight and not sit still blunting the keenness of his army and waiting for Vitellius himself to arrive from Gaul. **3** Paulinus, however, argued that all the enemy's fighting forces were there, and complete, whereas

Otho could expect reinforcements from Moesia and Pannonia not less than his present army, provided he waited and decided his strategy by the time best for them, not their opponents. 4 If his troops were confident now when their numbers were small he would not find them less keen once they were reinforced, and he would fight with numerical advantage. 5 Apart from that, delay was in their favour, since they had everything they needed, and in plenty, but the enemy were based in hostile territory and would in time face problems of supply. Paulinus' arguments were supported by Marius Celsus. 6 Annius Gallus, under treatment after a fall from his horse, was not present. When Otho wrote to him he advised against haste, saying he should wait for the army from Moesia, which was already on the march. None of these convinced Otho, and those who were urging him to fight had their way.

9.1 Various authorities give various reasons for his decision. The so-called Praetorians, who form the emperor's bodyguard, were having their first taste of real war, and missing the amusements, festivals, and civilian life-style of Rome. It was clearly difficult to control their impatience to fight, and they imagined they would roll up the enemy in their first charge. 2 It seems also that Otho himself could no longer stand the uncertainty, nor, being soft and out of his element, tolerate the hard thinking demanded by critical decisions – worn out by anxiety he could not wait to cover his eyes, like a man on the edge of a precipice, and leave the outcome to chance. 3 This is the explanation given by the orator Secundus, who was Otho's secretary. 4 I have heard from others that in both armies there were many movements towards reconciliation, and specifically to come to terms and name as emperor the best man among the generals present, or, failing that, to call a meeting of the Senate and leave the choice to it. 5 And it is not improbable, given the scant respect felt for both of those who were then called emperor, that such considerations did occur to those who were true, hardy, right-thinking soldiers: once, because of Marius and Sulla, then because of Caesar and Pompey the citizens had endured pitiable sufferings and inflicted them on each other; it would be terrible, unpardonable folly to endure these now while offering the empire as cashbox to fund the drunken gluttony of Vitellius or the pampered profligacy of Otho. 6 These sources suspect that Celsus, realizing this, suggested delay, hoping that the issue would be decided without the tough business of battle, and that Otho, fearing it, hastened the engagement.

10.1 He himself returned to Brixellum – a second mistake, not only because he removed from his troops the fear of shame and zeal for distinction they would have felt fighting before his eyes, but he took with him as bodyguard his toughest and keenest cavalry and infantry, and, so to speak, took the edge off his army. **2** At this same time there was combat on the Po, which Caecina tried to bridge in the face of resistance and assaults from Otho's troops. **3** When these proved ineffective they loaded their boats with pine covered with sulphur and pitch, but a sudden breeze came up while they were crossing the channel and the material prepared against the enemy was fanned into flame. **4** First smoke arose then a clear blaze; taken by surprise, jumping into the water, capsizing their boats, they exposed themselves defenceless to their jeering opponents. **5** In addition the Germans attacked Otho's gladiators from an island in the river and defeated them, inflicting heavy losses.

11.1 These setbacks inspired Otho's troops at Bedriacum with an angry passion for battle, and Proculus led them out. He pitched camp ten kilometres from Bedriacum, with such ludicrous incompetence that, even though it was spring and there were many creeks and permanent rivers in the surrounding flat land, he was embarrassed by lack of water. **2** The next day he wanted to advance and challenge the enemy. The distance was at least twenty kilometres, and Paulinus objected. He believed they should wait and not tire themselves too soon, nor, straight after a march, join battle with soldiers who had been armed and drawn up in their own good time while they were covering a considerable distance encumbered by transport animals and non-combatants. **3** They were still debating the point when a mounted courier (one of those they call 'Numidians') arrived with written orders from Otho not to waste time waiting but to advance against the enemy immediately. **4** They therefore broke camp and moved off. The news of their approach alarmed Caecina, who hastily abandoned the river and his work on the bridge and returned to his camp. **5** Most of the soldiers were already armed and being given the password issued by Valens, and while the units were being assigned their positions a picked force of cavalry was sent out.

12.1 For some reason a rumour surfaced and spread among the front ranks of Otho's troops that Vitellius' generals were about to change sides and join them. Consequently when the enemy came close they called them comrades and greeted them as friends. **2** The response to their greeting, however, was not that of friends, but a bellicose roar of rage which dismayed those who had welcomed them, while the rest suspected them of treachery. This threw them out for a start, when the enemy were already hand to hand. **3** From then on there was no system in anything they did. The transport animals, roaming loose among the soldiers, caused them endless confusion, and their lines were fragmented by the terrain – it was a network of ditches and channels, and, warily skirting these, they were forced to fight as many unco-ordinated units. **4** Only two legions (as the Romans call their regiments), Vitellius' 'Spoiler' and Otho's 'Support', having deployed onto a wide, treeless plain, met in complete formation and fought a protracted regular engagement. **5** Otho's men were vigorous and fearless, but this was their first experience of warfare and battle; Vitellius' were veterans of many a struggle but with their best years already behind them. **6** When Otho's troops charged they drove Vitellius' back, captured their eagle, and annihilated their front ranks. Stung by rage and shame Vitellius' legion counterattacked, killing the legionary legate Orfidius and seizing many of their standards. **7** Against the gladiators, who had a reputation for skill and courage in close combat, Alfenus Varus sent in the Batavians, as they are called (they are the best cavalry in Germany, and come from an island formed by the Rhine). **8** A few of the gladiators stood their ground, but most of them took flight towards the river where they blundered into the enemy cohorts stationed there and, trying to hold them off, were killed to a man. **9** Most shameful of all was the part played in the battle by the Praetorian Guards. They did not even wait for the enemy to close with them but, breaking in flight through the ranks that were still intact, filled them too with fear and confusion. **10** Yet in spite of everything many of Otho's troops gained the upper hand in their own sector and forced their way back to the camp through the victorious enemy.

13.1 Two of Otho's generals, Proculus and Paulinus, were afraid to go back with them. They turned aside, nervous of the soldiers, who were already fastening the blame on their commanders. **2** In Bedriacum Annius Gallus took in those who were re-uniting after the battle and tried to encourage them by saying it had been a close run thing and at many points they had had the better of the enemy. **3** Marius Celsus, however, having called the officers together, told them they should think of the public good. 'After a disaster of such proportions and the slaughter of so many Romans,' he said, 'not even Otho, if he is a good man, will want to try fortune further. **4** Look at Cato and Scipio – after their defeat at Pharsalus they refused to surrender to Caesar and are held responsible for the pointless death of so many brave men in Libya, and they were fighting for the freedom of Rome. **5** In most regards fortune affects everyone the same, but there is one thing it cannot take from good men, and that is their ability to weigh a situation rationally even after a setback.' His argument convinced the officers, **6** and when they had sounded the soldiers and found them in favour of peace, and Titianus had said they should send a delegation to arrange an accord, it was decided that Celsus and Gallus should go and confer with Caecina and Valens. **7** On their way they were met by centurions who told them that Vitellius' army was already on the march towards Bedriacum, and that the generals had sent them to propose an accord. **8** Celsus and Gallus applauded their initiative, and told them to turn back to meet Caecina together. **9** Their approach to the troops, however, proved dangerous for Celsus. The cavalry who had previously been routed in the ambush happened to be riding in front, and when they saw Celsus coming towards them they immediately raised a shout and charged him. **10** The centurions posted themselves in front of him and held them off; other officers roared at them not to touch him. Caecina, informed of the confrontation, rode up and quelled the unruly cavalry in short order, then, having greeted Celsus amicably, went on with him to Bedriacum. **11** In the meantime, however, Titianus was regretting having sent out the delegation. He once more manned the walls with his toughest fighters and called on the others to support him. **12** But when Caecina rode up and stretched out his right hand, no one opposed him. Those on the walls shouted greetings to the soldiers, others opened the gates and went out to join them as they approached. **13** Not one of the defenders offered violence. Rather, they shook hands like old friends and all of them joined Vitellius and took the oath in his name.

14.1 This is the account of the battle given by most of those who were present, although they admit that not even they had clear knowledge of the details because of its confused and irregular character. **2** Later, as I was travelling across the plain, Mestrius Florus (a Roman of consular rank, and one of those who had at the time accompanied Otho not from choice but by necessity) pointed out an ancient temple and said that when he went there after the battle he had seen a pile of corpses so high that those on top were touching the pediments. **3** Although he had tried, he could neither discover an explanation himself nor hear one from anybody else. It was natural that more should die after defeat in civil war, where no prisoners were taken since they were no use to their captors, but there was no apparent reason why they should be collected and piled up like that.

15.1 As often happens after momentous events, the first news to reach Otho was inconclusive; then wounded arrived from the battle with eye-witness reports. Perhaps no one should be surprised at his friends, who would not let him lose heart and encouraged him to bear up, but the reaction of his soldiers surpassed all belief. **2** Not one of them deserted or went over to the victors or was seen looking after his own hide and giving up his leader as beyond hope, but all of them alike went to his door, called him emperor, shouted pleas and entreaties when he came out, touched his hands, fell at his feet, wept, begged him not to abandon them, not to betray them to the enemy, but to use them in his cause, body and soul, as long as they had breath. They all pleaded with him thus, **3** but an ordinary legionary drew his sword and saying 'Caesar, every man of us is ready to do this for you,' killed himself. **4** None of this swayed Otho, whose eyes ranged over the crowd while his expression remained calm and unclouded. 'Comrades,' he said, 'when I see men like you holding me worthy of such honour, this day seems happier to me than the one on which you first made me emperor. **5** But do not deprive me of a still greater honour: to die well for the sake of so many true Romans. If I deserved to be emperor I cannot grudge my life to the land of my birth. **6** I know that the enemy have won no sure, final victory. I have reports that our army from Moesia is already coming down to the Adriatic and is only a few days' march away. Asia, Syria, Egypt and the forces fighting the Jews are on our side; the Senate is behind our lines, and the wives and children of our opponents. **7** But this is not a war in defence of Italy against Hannibal or Pyrrhus or the Cimbri. It is Roman against Roman, and both sides, win or lose, are doing wrong to their country. The triumph of the victor is defeat for the nation. **8** I have given the matter some thought, and take my word that the nobler choice for me is dying now, not ruling. I cannot see how I would do more good for Rome by winning than by giving up my life for peace and concord and to spare Italy the sight of another day like this.'

16.1 Even after this some tried to oppose him and talk him round, but Otho never wavered. He told his friends and the men of consular rank who were there to leave Bedriacum, and for those who went he wrote letters to local authorities to ensure they would be sent on their way safely and with honour. **2** Then he called in his nephew Cocceianus, a boy still in his teens, and told him not to lose heart or be afraid of Vitellius, whose mother, wife and children he had watched over like members of his own family. **3** 'I wanted,' he said, 'to adopt you as my son, but I put it off so that you could rule with me if I conquered but not fall with me if I failed. **4** Now listen to a final word of advice: do not quite forget, nor too well remember, that you had an uncle who was Caesar.' **5** Not long after this he heard a confused shouting at his door. It was the soldiers, who were threatening to kill the departing senators if they did not stay there but went off and deserted the emperor. **6** Concerned for their safety he came out again. There were no bland entreaties now. His face was set, and fixing stony eyes on the ringleaders he cowed the soldiers and they melted away in terror.

17.1 By now it was evening. He felt thirsty and drank a little water, then took his two swords and examined the blades of both for a long time. Having given one back he put the other under his arm and called his servants. **2** He spoke to them affectionately and gave them money, more to some, less to others, not as if making free with someone else's property but paying careful regard to what was reasonable and deserved. **3** After he had dismissed them he spent the rest of the night in such calm repose that it was clear to the attendants that he was sleeping soundly. **4** At daybreak he called the freedman who had helped him manage the departure of the senators and told him to find out how they had fared. When he heard that those who left had been given everything they asked for, he said 'You now, go and show yourself to the soldiers if you don't want a nasty death at their hands for abetting me in mine.' **5** The freedman left, and Otho, holding the sword upright with both hands, fell on it, feeling the pain only long enough to give a single groan. Those outside knew what it meant. **6** His slaves raised a cry of sorrow, and in an instant the whole camp and the town were swept by the sound of mourning. **7** The soldiers rushed shouting to his door, reviling themselves in their bitter anguish for not having watched over their emperor and prevented him from sacrificing his life for them. **8** Although the enemy were near not one of his followers left him. They built a pyre, and having adorned his body carried it out with military honours, and those who were first to put the bier on their shoulders and took it to the pyre were proud men. **9** The others threw themselves on the corpse and kissed the wound or clasped its hands or, if they were too far away, went down on their knees. **10** Some of them put their torches to the pyre then killed themselves, although there was no indication that they had received any favour from the dead emperor or were afraid of suffering at the victor's hands. **11** It seems, indeed, that there never was a king or tyrant who felt such a consuming passion to rule as their passion to serve and be ruled by Otho. **12** This fierce attachment did not leave them even after his death, but persisted and finally transformed itself into implacable hatred for Vitellius.

18.1 (That story, however, will be told in its own time.) They buried Otho's ashes in a tomb whose modest stone and laconic epitaph were devoid of pretension. **2** I saw it when I was in Brixellum: a simple monument with an epitaph which reads in translation 'Sacred to the spirit of Marcus Otho'. **3** When Otho died he was thirty-seven years old and had been emperor for three months, and those he left praising his death were neither fewer nor worse than those who condemned his life. He may have lived as licentiously as Nero, but he died more nobly. **4** Plotius, joint commander of the Praetorian Guard, ordered the soldiers to swear an oath to Vitellius immediately, but they reacted with anger. **5** Having heard that a few men of senatorial rank were still present, they allowed them all to leave with the exception of Verginius Rufus, whom they embarrassed by going armed to his quarters and asking, or demanding, that he should become emperor, or negotiate on their behalf. **6** He, however, thought it madness to accept from his troops in defeat the supreme power which he had previously refused when they had offered it as victors, and, apprehensive about negotiating with the German legions, who felt he had often forced unwelcome decisions upon them, he slipped away unseen through another door. **7** When the soldiers realized this, they agreed to the oath and joined Caecina, who took no reprisals.

Commentary

The *Life* of Galba

1.1. On Greek mercenaries, see Parke, *Greek Mercenary Soldiers*.

Iphicrates (c. 415-353 BC), an Athenian, was one of the most distinguished and innovative mercenary leaders of the early fourth century BC; Parke describes his career, pp. 50-7, 77-82, 105-6.

'**be moved like a single body by the will of their commander**': compare Iphicrates' own opinion (Polyaenus III 9.22), 'He compared the organization of armies to the human body: he called the phalanx its chest, the light-armed its hands, the cavalry its feet, and the general its head.'

2. Aemilius Paulus: as consul for the second time, 168 BC, he defeated Perseus, the last king of Macedonia, at Pydna, and so ended a war which had lasted three years, largely because of the incompetence of the previous commanders. Plutarch wrote his *Life* (paired with Timoleon), and devotes nearly half of it to describing the Pydna campaign; he gives Paulus' words there (13.6) as 'they should not meddle nor have any thought except for each to keep his body and equipment ready and use his sword like a Roman when their general gave them the chance.' Livy (XLIV 34.3) makes him give similar instructions. Both Livy and Plutarch presumably drew on Polybius' account, which does not survive.

3. Plato: No surviving work of Plato's contains exactly these phrases, but Plutarch is presumably thinking of *Republic* II 375e, where he says that the 'guardians' of the ideal state, like good watch-dogs, should have both 'passion of spirit' and 'philosophic temper'; cf. also III 410d-e, 411e-412a, on the mental and physical education which the 'guardians' should receive, and IV 442b-c, on how the warrior 'guardians' would obey the instructions of the 'philosopher' rulers.

5. Alexander the Great died in Babylon on 10th June 323 BC, and his generals almost at once began quarrelling about who should be his successor and control his empire; the wars of the 'Successors' lasted until 281 BC, when the last two surviving generals, Seleucus and Lysimachus, fought at Corupedium in south-west Asia Minor. Lysimachus was defeated and killed, and Seleucus was murdered early in 280.

Demades (c. 380-319 BC), a prominent pro-Macedonian politician at Athens, noted for his quick wit and his venality. Plutarch also quotes this saying of his in *Moralia* 181F (*Sayings of Alexander* 34), and, in the *Life* of Phocion 22, says Demades warned the Athenians not to believe the first report they had of Alexander's death, for if it were true 'the whole world would long since stink of the corpse.' In *On the Fortune of Alexander* 4 (*Mor.* 336F) Plutarch attributes the comparison with the blinded Cyclops to Leosthenes, the Athenian leader in the Greek War against the Macedonians (the Lamian War) immediately after Alexander's death.

The **Cyclops**, Polyphemus, was blinded by Odysseus (Homer, *Odyssey* IX 371-419).

6. the 'War of the Titans': Hesiod, *Theogony* 132-8, lists the Titans, the children of Gaea and Uranus (i.e. Earth and Heaven), of whom the leader was the youngest, Kronos, who overthrew his father to become the supreme ruler; he then begat children, of whom the youngest was Zeus, who in turn overthrew Kronos and his fellow Titans in a 'titanic' struggle which lasted for ten years, described in *Theogony* 617-735.

not so much through hunger for power: this is Plutarch's particular interpretation of the upheavals of 68 and 69, which lays the blame primarily not on the ambition of the leaders, or even of prominent supporters, who hoped to gain wealth and influence, but on the indiscipline and greed of the soldiers.

as nail drives out nail: already proverbial for Aristotle, *Politics* V 11.6.1314a5, 'Wicked men are useful for wickedness – for a nail (is driven out) with a nail, as the saying is'. Plutarch may allude to it, *Advice on Keeping Well* 11 (*Mor.* 127F), 'with the proverb as support...expecting to drive out wine with wine and hangover with hangover'.

7. Dionysius: presumably the Elder Dionysius, who ruled as tyrant of Syracuse from 405 to 367 BC. Plutarch relates other sayings of his, *Sayings of Kings and Commanders, Mor.* 175C-176C.

Polyphron: The name is not in the manuscripts, which only have 'Pheraean', but it is an almost certain supplement, both for grammar and sense. Jason, the powerful tyrant of Pherae, was murdered in 370 BC, and succeeded by his brothers Polydorus and Polyphron; Polydorus died very soon after, and Polyphron within a year was killed by Alexander of Pherae. See Xenophon, *Hellenica* VI 4.33-5 and Plutarch, *Pelopidas* 29.

king of tragedy: i.e. an actor, who plays the part on stage, and loses it when the play ends. Philostratus, *Life of Apollonius* V 13.2, makes Apollonius use the same analogy.

8. in shorter space: Nero committed suicide on 9th June 68, after the Praetorian Guard had proclaimed Galba emperor (2.1; Suet. *Nero* 48-9, 57.1 with Warmington's note); the Rhine legions proclaimed Vitellius emperor in the night of 1st-2nd January 69 (22); Galba was murdered and Otho proclaimed on 15th January (24.3) – thus giving four emperors in a little over seven months, though Vitellius did not actually arrive in Rome until July 69 (Tac. *H*. II 87-91, esp. 91.1). Alternatively, one might reckon from Galba's arrival in Rome, probably in October 68 (15.5), to the proclamation of Vespasian in Egypt on 1st July 69, but that has the similar drawback that Vespasian did not arrive in Rome until some time in 70, and also, if it is correct that Plutarch wrote the *Lives* of Galba and Otho under the Flavian emperors, it is not likely that he would want to include Vespasian among the ephemeral 'kings of tragedy'.

the Palatine: one of the seven hills of Rome, overlooking the Forum. Augustus' house was there, and later emperors extended it so that the imperial residence filled the whole Palatine. From this, all imperial residences came to be called *palatia*, 'palaces'.

9. First to fall: Nymphidius Sabinus, chapters 2, 13-15.

a noble deed: Plutarch is convinced that the rebellion against Nero was justified, for overthrowing a tyrant (cf. *Antony* 87, at end). Also, of course, if it had not occurred, Vespasian and his sons would not have become emperors.

act of betrayal: Nymphidius, as commander of the emperor's guard, was particularly bound to be loyal to the emperor.

2.1. Nymphidius Sabinus: Son of Nymphidia, a daughter of Callistus (9.2), who was an influential freedman of Gaius Caligula and then of Claudius. His father is unknown: popular rumour named a gladiator, Martianus (9.3), while Nymphidius himself claimed that his father was Caligula (9.1; Tac. *A*. XV 72.2). Since he claimed that Caligula (born AD 12) had engendered him as a teenager, he was presumably born about AD 30. Nero appointed him Praetorian Prefect, as Tigellinus' colleague, in 65, after the suppression of the Pisonian conspiracy, and also gave him consular ornaments for his part in putting the conspiracy down (Tac. loc. cit.). Unfortunately there are lacunae in Tacitus' text, where he gave a character sketch of Nymphidius on his first appearance in his history, thus depriving us of most of the details. See 8-9 and 13-14, below.

as I have said: obviously in the lost *Life* of Nero, where he probably described the events preceding and surrounding Nero's deposition and suicide in detail. Here he gives only a résumé.

Tigellinus: Ofonius Tigellinus was brought up in the household of the sisters of Caligula, and in 39 was exiled for alleged adultery with the eldest of them, Agrippina, the mother of Nero. He was recalled under Claudius, and became influential with Nero through his interest in chariot-racing and horse-breeding. Nero appointed him Praetorian Prefect, with Faenius Rufus as colleague, after the death in 62 of Burrus, Agrippina's supporter. Tigellinus played a leading and brutal part in suppressing the Pisonian conspiracy, in which his colleague Faenius Rufus had been involved, and received exceptional honours from Nero for his services (Tac. *A.* XV 58-72). Despite this, in the crisis of 68 he allegedly betrayed Nero (17.4, Tac. *H.* I 72, Jos. *Jewish War* IV 493), though the details are unknown; he certainly did nothing to rally the Praetorians to support the emperor. For his life under Galba and suicide under Otho, see 17, and *Otho* 2, and the notes there.

Praetorian Guard: nine cohorts, of 500 men each, quartered in barracks in a strongly fortified camp on the edge of Rome. They were the best paid soldiers in the empire, receiving approximately twice the pay of the legionaries, and had much better conditions. They were by far the largest single body of troops in Italy. Usually they were commanded jointly by two Prefects, as a precaution against treachery (though both Prefects had joined the successful conspiracy against Caligula in AD 41, and both betrayed Nero); the Prefects were almost always equestrians, i.e. of the highest Roman class outside the Senate, and the Prefecture of the Guard ranked with the Prefecture of Egypt (which was always governed by an equestrian) as the highest post a non-senator could attain. Like all officers, the Prefects were appointed directly by the emperor, and held their post at his pleasure. In general, see Webster, *Roman Imperial Army* 96-8 (who, however, is wrong to suppose, p. 97, that there were 1,000 per cohort before Vitellius).

Nero had abandoned all hope and was clearly planning escape to Egypt: Dio LXIII 27.2 states 'when he had been abandoned by all alike, he planned to kill the senators and burn down the city, and to sail to Alexandria'; Suet. *Nero* 47.2 that among his last plans was 'to pray that he might be allowed to be Prefect of Egypt'.

alleging that the emperor was...already in flight: Tac. *H.* I 5, 'The city garrison...had been induced to desert Nero more by cunning and suggestion than from any inclination of its own'.

to proclaim Galba emperor: the Praetorians had already been the first to proclaim Caligula in 37, Claudius in 41 (when they forced the Senate unwillingly to accept their choice), and Nero in 54, as emperors, and in each case the Senate had ratified their choice. The new factors in 68 were, first, that the previous emperor was still alive when his successor was proclaimed, so that the Guard was in open rebellion, and secondly, that Galba had not the least family connection with his predecessor.

2. He promised every soldier of the Guard…7,500 denarii, and 1,250 to the legions abroad: Augustus, in his will, had left 250 *denarii* to each guardsman and 75 to each legionary (Tac. *A.* I 8), which presumably Tiberius paid; Tiberius, in his will, left the same amounts (Dio LIX 2.1-3), but since the Senate declared his will null and void, the bequests would not have been paid, had Caligula not paid them as a gratuity, and added a further 250 *denarii* for each guardsman (Dio loc. cit.), making this the first time an emperor paid a donative at his accession. Claudius, who owed the throne and probably his life to the Guard's support, paid a donative of either 3,750 (Suet. *Claud.* 10.4) or 5,000 (Jos. *Jewish Ant.* XIX 247) *denarii* per man, so that Suetonius, ignoring Caligula's payment, claims he was 'the first of the Caesars to win the soldiers' loyalty with an actual price'; Josephus (loc. cit.) adds that Claudius promised a similar payment to all the armies. Nero, though his accession was practically unopposed, made the same payment as Claudius (Tac. *A.* XII 69). So the Praetorians could reasonably expect a considerably larger payment for the apparently much riskier service of deserting the emperor who was on the spot and proclaiming a new one. The annual pay for a Praetorian at this time was probably either 375 or 450 *denarii* (Webster 97-8), so Nymphidius was offering them up to twenty years' pay at once. If there were 4,500 guardsmen then the donative, even ignoring the much higher amounts that would have been due to centurions and officers, would have amounted to 33,750,000 *denarii*, or about 100 tonnes of silver.

Legionaries at this time were paid 225 *denarii* per year, so Nymphidius was offering about 5 $\frac{1}{2}$ year's pay as donative. There were 27 legions at the beginning of 68, with a nominal strength of 5,200 men each. Doubtless most were under strength, but since their cavalry, centurions and officers were paid much more than the private soldiers, it is reasonable to take the full strength as basis for working out the cost of the promised donative. For the total force of about 140,000 men, it would amount to 175 million *denarii*, or nearly 600 tonnes of silver. There would also have to be some payments to the soldiers in the auxiliary forces in the provinces, and especially in the urban cohorts in Rome, who from earlier emperors had received half as much per man in donatives as the Praetorians had.

'Palace' and 'Praetorian' Guards: from the beginning of Augustus' reign, there was always one praetorian cohort on guard at the palace. The guard was called 'praetorian' because the basic meaning of *praetor* in Latin is 'commander', and each commander under the Republic had formed a bodyguard for himself of picked men from his forces. When Augustus had become the supreme and permanent commander, his guard was the only 'praetorian' guard.

sufferings infinitely greater than those inflicted by Nero: Suet. *Nero* 30 states that Nero used to praise and admire his uncle Gaius Caligula above all because Caligula had in a very short time spent the reserve of 675 million *denarii* which Tiberius had accumulated, and that Nero himself spent 200,000 *denarii* per day on entertaining Tiridates, king of Armenia, on his visit to Italy in AD 66, and gave him a parting gift of over 25 million.

3. the military deserted one in hope of reward, and killed the other when the hope proved false: compare Tac. *H.* I 5, 'The city garrison...now discovered that payment of the bounty promised in the name of Galba was not forthcoming', and I 18 (at the adoption of Piso), 'There is general agreement that it would have been quite possible to win the Praetorians over by a mere token act of generosity.' By 'the military', Plutarch here obviously means only the Praetorians; he ignores the resentment of the legions, especially those on the Rhine frontier (cf. 22-3).

4. they destroyed themselves by mutiny and betrayal before they ever touched their coveted prize: the Praetorians suffered heavy losses in fighting for Otho against the Vitellians, and after Otho's defeat at Bedriacum and suicide they were disbanded (Tac. *H.* II 67, Suet. *Vitell.* 10.1), and Vitellius formed a new Praetorian Guard from his own legions. The discharged guardsmen joined the Flavian forces (Tac. loc. cit.) and played a prominent part in the capture of Rome in December 69 (*H.* III 84); for their efforts, Mucianus, the Flavian commander, paid the survivors a donative of 25 *denarii* each (Dio LXV 22.2).

5. the historian proper: Plutarch uses the phrase 'pragmatic history' which Polybius (I 2.8) uses to describe his history, a thorough political and military account; Plutarch's aims are much more limited, for he only focusses on the personalities of the emperors and the events which directly affected them; on the other hand, he does not give a full biography, but omits almost everything about their earlier lives that is not relevant to their actions as rulers. His conception of biography here is much more limited than that which he applies in the *Parallel Lives*: for his conception of biography there, in contrast to history, see his own statements, *Nicias* 1.5, *Alexander* 1.

3.1. Sulpicius Galba: Suet. *Galba* 2.1-9.2. gives much more detail about Galba's ancestry and his life before his rebellion against Nero in April 68. See also Dio LXIV 1, and Tacitus' obituary, *H.* I 49.

the wealthiest: Tacitus loc. cit., 'he came of a family that could boast ancient nobility and great wealth'. Galba's stepmother, Livia Ocellina, was exceptionally rich, and adopted him in her will (Suet. *Galba* 3.7, 4.1).

the house of the Servii: Plutarch, like many Greeks in the Roman empire (even those who had Roman citizenship), found Roman names difficult (he wrote an essay, now lost, on the subject, *Moralia* (Loeb edn) vol. XV 17, no. 100). Galba's 'family' name was Sulpicius; 'Servius' was his *praenomen* ('fore-name'), so strictly it was his personal name; however, hardly any family except the Sulpicii used it, so it was almost as distinctive as the family name, and in fact Tacitus makes Otho use it in the same way, *H.* II 48, 'After all the Julians, Claudians and Servians he had been the first to win the imperial dignity'.

the prestige of high nobility: see Tac. *H.* I 49. Suet. *Galba* 3, gives details, and in 2 states that, after Galba became emperor, he set up his family tree in his *atrium*, in which he traced his ancestry on his father's side to Jupiter, and on his mother's to Pasiphae, the wife of Minos, the legendary king of Crete.

kinship with Catulus: Q. Lutatius Catulus (c. 121-61 or 60 BC), consul 78 BC, and charged with suppressing the attempt of his fellow consul, M. Aemilius Lepidus, to overthrow the constitutional and political changes which Sulla had introduced after his victory in 82, which he was only able to do with Pompey's help. In 69 BC he inaugurated the rebuilt temple of Jupiter on the Capitol, which had burnt down in 83. He was censor in 65-64, as colleague of Crassus. In 63 BC he was beaten by Julius Caesar in the election for the post of *Pontifex Maximus*, the chief priest. Plutarch praises him in *Crassus* 13 as 'the gentlest of the Romans', and in *Cato Minor* 16 says 'he had a great reputation for high character, as excelling all Romans in justice and moderation'. His younger contemporary, Cicero, always speaks of him with respect (e.g. *Pro Sestio* 101, *In Pisonem* 6).

2. related to Livia: Plutarch is probably mistaken, perhaps by confusing Livia Ocellina, Galba's stepmother and adoptive mother, with Livia Drusilla (58 BC-AD 29), Augustus' second wife; Galba's official name was L. Livius Ocella at least in his consulship in 33 (Sherk p. 53), and L. Livius was used of him by the Prefect of Egypt on 6th July 68, probably because an up-to-date list of names and titles had not yet reached Egypt in the four weeks since Nero's suicide (Braund no. 600). Suetonius says explicitly (*Galba* 2) that Galba was in no way related to the house of the Caesars, which seems to exclude any relationship with Livia, who was Nero's great-great-grand-mother; however, he also says (ibid. 5.2), 'before all others he paid court to Livia Augusta, by whose favour he gained great influence while she lived and would have been enriched through her will on her death' (if Tiberius had not deprived him of the legacy), and this close association may also help to explain Plutarch's mistake.

Caesar: Augustus (63 BC-AD 14), sole ruler of the Roman world after the defeat of Antony in 31 BC.

his consulship: AD 33, for the first six months of the year. How Livia supported him is a mystery, since she died four years earlier.

from the Palatine: normally, the consul entered on his office on 1st

January with auspices and other ceremonies in his own house (Livy XXI 63.10); to perform them and to make one's first public appearance as consul in the emperor's house was an exceptional distinction. Suetonius (*Galba* 6.1) points out the ominous coincidence that Nero's father preceded him as consul, and Otho's father followed him.

3. commanded with distinction in Germany: Suet. *Galba* 6.2 gives the circumstances of his appointment by Caligula in 39 to command the legions in Upper Germany, and instances of his severity; cf. also Dio LX 8.7 for some of his military successes, and Tac. *H*. I 49. He remained in this post till 43, when he accompanied Claudius in the invasion of Britain (Suet. *Galba* 7.2).

proconsul of Libya: i.e. of the Roman province 'Africa'. This province and 'Asia' were, from Augustus' reign onwards, reserved for ex-consuls, normally chosen by lot, and the governorship, which with rare exceptions was limited to one year, generally marked the climax and end of a successful senatorial career. Suet. *Galba* 7.3 states that Galba was appointed without resort to the lot, and governed Africa for two years (probably mid-44 to mid-46) in order to settle the state of the province which was troubled both by internal strife and by barbarian raids, a task he performed successfully, with severity but also justice.

4. outmoded reputation...of self-discipline and moderation: Suetonius gives examples (*Galba* 6.3, 7.4, 9.2). Cf. Tac. *H*. I 5,'There were rumours, too, about Galba's brutality and miserliness. His strictness...now irritated men who would have nothing to do with the discipline of the past'.

5. Nero...sent him to Spain as governor: in 60, to be *legatus pro praetore* of Tarraconensis, the most important of the three Spanish provinces and the only one with a legionary garrison (4.3, Suet. *Galba* 8.1-9.1, Dio LXIII 23).

not yet learned to fear citizens: by 60, Nero had murdered his mother, in 59 (Tac. *A*. XIV 1-10); other notable victims had been his cousin Marcus Junius Silanus, in 54 (*A*. XIII 1), and his adoptive brother Britannicus, in 55 (ibid. 15-17); other relations, Faustus Cornelius Sulla and Rubellius Plautus, had been banished for trumped-up reasons (ibid. 47, XIV 22).

held in high regard: cf. the conclusion of Tacitus' obituary, with the epigrammatic and practically untranslatable words, *maior privato visus dum privatus fuit et omnium consensu capax imperii nisi imperasset*, translated by Wellesley (Penguin), 'so long as he was a subject, he seemed too great a man to be one, and by common consent possessed the makings of a ruler – had he never ruled'.

his advanced age: our sources for Galba's date of birth are irreconcilable. Suet. *Galba* 4.1 states he was born on 24th December 'in the consulship of

Marcus Valerius Messala and Gnaeus Lentulus', i.e. 3 BC, but states that at death (he was murdered on 15th January AD 69) he was in his 73rd year (ibid. 23), which would mean he was born in 5 BC; he also states (*Nero* 40.5) that the Delphic oracle warned Nero to beware of the 73rd year, referring to Galba (and not, as Nero of course supposed, to himself). This presumably implies that Galba was 72 ('in his 73rd year') at the time of his rebellion, at the beginning of April 68, and therefore was born in 6 BC. Dio LXVI 6.5[2] states that Galba lived 72 years, 23 days, which, with inclusive reckoning, also gives 24th December 5 BC as date of birth. Tacitus, in his obituary (*H.* I 49), states 'in the course of seventy-three years he had lived a successful life', which suggests 6 BC as year of birth. Plutarch himself (8.1) says that Galba was 73 in summer or autumn 68, which would mean he was born in 7 BC. It is most likely that Dio is right, with his precise details of the length of Galba's life, though it is hard to see why Suetonius should have given the wrong consuls, and have missed the ominous fact that Galba was born in the year which opened with Augustus' twelfth consulship. If Dio is right, then Galba was 63 when he was sent to govern Tarraconensis.

4.1. procurators: men of equestrian rank, appointed directly by the emperor to look after his affairs, especially his financial affairs, in the provinces. They were not under the governor's control, and relations between them and the governor were often strained (cf. Tac. *Agr.* 9.4, 15.2, *A.* XII 60, XIV 38, *H.* I 12, Suet. *Galba* 9.5, Plut. *Galba* 19.1).

plundering the provincials: on Nero's need for money, especially after the Great Fire of Rome in 64, see Tac. *A.* XV 45, Suet. *Nero* 30-3, Dio LXIII 22.1-2.

2. satirical verses against Nero: similar verses were posted up in Rome, but Nero ignored them (Suet. *Nero* 39).

3. Julius Vindex: the details of Vindex' career, and the aims of his rebellion, have provoked much scholarly debate, which cannot be summarized here. Dio (or rather his epitomator Xiphilinus) says 'he was descended from the Aquitanian royal race, but by paternal descent a Roman senator, powerful in body and intelligent in mind, experienced in matters of war and ready to dare every great enterprise; he had exceeding love of liberty and honour; he was in charge of the Gauls' (LXIII 22.1[2]). No other details of his career are known, nor is there any explicit evidence for which of the four Gallic provinces he governed. Aquitania, however, can be eliminated, since its governor appealed to Galba for help after Vindex' rising (Suet. *Galba* 9.4); Suetonius (*Nero* 40.1) says he was governor *pro praetore*, which probably means he governed an 'imperial' province (i.e. either Belgica or

Lugdunensis) as *legatus Augusti pro praetore*, and not the 'senatorial' province, Narbonensis, as 'proconsul'; Plutarch's word for 'governor' is the Greek equivalent of *praetor*, not of 'proconsul', which reinforces the argument. It is impossible to decide for certain between Belgica and Lugdunensis, though practically all modern writers assume he governed Lugdunensis – if so, it is strange that he was unable to get the support of the provincial capital, Lugdunum (Lyons), which he had to besiege, but failed to capture (Tac. *H.* I 65). It is even possible that Suetonius and Plutarch both wrote non-technically, and that Vindex was proconsul of Narbonensis; certainly he was supported by tribes and communities in all four Gallic provinces. Despite Sutherland, *RIC* I^2 pp. 198-9, 206-9, no coins are known which might have been struck for Vindex; those attributed to him were all, or almost all, struck for Galba.

rebelled against Nero: the fullest, but still very inadequate, account is in the fragments of Dio LXIII 22-4; other details in Suet. *Nero* 40-1, *Galba* 9.2, Tac. *H.* I 8, 51, 53, 65, IV 17, 69, Jos. *Jewish War* IV 440, Plut. *Galba* 6.4, Philostratus, *Life of Apollonius* V 10. For a recent and thorough discussion see Barbara Levick, 'L. Verginius Rufus and the four emperors' (though some of her conclusions are debatable).

4. before the outbreak of the revolt, a letter from Vindex: cf. Jos. *Jewish War* IV 440-3, who implies that Vespasian, in Palestine, knew of Vindex' revolt before the end of the winter 67/68. For preparations for rebellion in the Roman empire, and letters seeking support, see Ramsay MacMullen, 'How to revolt in the Roman empire'.

5. When Vindex openly declared war: Nero heard the news of the rebellion on the anniversary of his mother's murder (Suet. *Nero* 40.4). He killed his mother during the *Quinquatrus* (Tac. *A.* XIV 12.1), which were celebrated from 19th to 23rd March. Since the news must have taken some days to travel from Gaul to Naples, where Nero was, Vindex' rebellion took place in the first half of March; J.B. Hainsworth, 'Verginius and Vindex', 87, very plausibly suggested that it began publicly on the Ides of March, the 15th; cf. Murison, *Galba, Otho and Vitellius* 4-5.

accept the leadership: all the propaganda for the rebellion, up to the time that the Senate voted the imperial powers to Galba (2.1, 7.2), is republican in character and avoids any suggestion that there should be a new monarch to replace Nero; ostensibly, at any rate, Vindex was calling on Galba to lend his reputation and talents as a leader, not to set himself up as a rival emperor. Cf. Dio LXIII 23; Suet. *Galba* 9.2.

which, he said, had 100,000 men under arms: the usual optimistic exaggeration of rebels. However, Vindex must have raised very large levies, for Plutarch says (7.4) that 20,000 of Vindex' men were killed at the battle at Vesontio; though Tacitus writes (*H.* I 51) of 'the destruction of Julius Vindex and all his force', obviously many more survived and fled than were killed, and besides those at Vesontio, others of his men were besieging Lugdunum (ibid. 65), and no doubt there were other detachments of which we are ignorant. The rebellion was obviously a serious matter, much more substantial, at least in numbers, than that of Florus and Sacrovir in AD 21 (Tac. *A.* III 40-6).

6. consulted his friends: his *consilium*, composed of his staff and the friends he had taken with him to the province as advisers and assistants.

7. Titus Vinius: see 12, for his career and character. Tac. *H.* I 48, gives the same details in very similar words.

the personal guard: the phrase Plutarch uses normally means 'Praetorian Guard', which, under the empire, was restricted to the emperor. Vinius was commander, *legatus legionis*, of the only legion in Spain, *VI Victrix*, and it must be this legion to which Plutarch, in non-technical language, is referring.

'Galba, what kind of plan etc.': ancient historians and biographers used great freedom in adapting or inventing speeches to suit particular occasions (cf. e.g. 22.4-5), and there is no reason to believe that Vinius spoke in precisely these or even similar terms. In particular, the neat antithesis between 'you as ruler rather than Nero as tyrant' betrays them as invented, since Vindex, and Galba as well, took up arms, ostensibly at least, to restore the Republic, not to make Galba emperor. If the common view, based on the usually accepted correction in 7.5, that Vinius was in Rome when Nero committed suicide were correct, this advice could not have been given as late as late March 68, after Vindex' open rebellion: if Vinius had arrived in Rome after the rebellion had begun, and after Nero had taken steps to remove Galba (Suet. *Galba* 9.5, cf. 10.6), he, like Icelus (7.1 note), would have been arrested, and would not have been free to move around the city. However, there are strong grounds for rejecting the correction (see note on 7.5). For the phrase, cf. Tac. *H.* II 77, 'those who deliberate have rebelled' (Mucianus to Vespasian).

5.1. the date: Dio LXIV 6.5^2 states that Galba lived for 72 years and 23 days. The number of days, at any rate, is correct by inclusive reckoning for the space from his birthday, 24th December, to the day of his murder, 15th January. Dio goes on, that he ruled for nine months and 13 days. This must again be inclusive reckoning, and places the date of Galba's public proclamation on 3rd April 68. This was an auspicious day, since it was the festival of Hercules Victor, and *Hercules Adsertor* ('the giver of freedom') duly appears as one of the types of the 'anonymous' coins struck for Galba in the period from his revolt until he knew of his acceptance as emperor by the Senate (Sutherland, *RIC* I² p. 207, no. 49). In general on Galba's revolt and aims, see Murison, *Galba, Otho and Vitellius*, chapter 3, though he shares the mistaken belief that, from the start, the movement was simply meant to replace Nero with Galba.

confer freedom: cf. Suet. *Galba* 10.1, 'as though going to spend time on manumission he ascended the tribunal'. A Roman who wished to free a slave in full legal form, which was important for the ex-slave's legal and economic rights, had to approach either a praetor in Rome or a provincial governor and request him to perform the ceremony (cf. Pliny, *Ep.* VII 16.4); for the details, see Buckland, *The Roman Law of Slavery* 441-2, 451-2. Since manumission granted freedom from the despotic power of the slave-owner, and turned the slave into a free Roman, the symbolism is obvious. The ceremony perhaps took place at Carthago Nova (Cartagena – cf. Suet. *Galba* 9.2), but more probably in the provincial capital, Tarraco (Tarragona).

all of them...hailed him emperor: similarly Suet. *Galba* 10.1, 'he was hailed emperor'; Suetonius, however, puts the acclamation after Galba's speech, not, like Plutarch, as a spontaneous expression as soon as he appeared.

2. he refused to accept the title: all the sources, Plutarch, Suetonius (*Galba* 10.1), Dio (LXIII 29.6), and the coins (Sutherland, *RIC* I² 197-9, catalogued 203-9; despite *RIC*, these were struck in Spain, for Galba), agree that Galba professed to be subordinate to the wishes of Senate and Roman People, and only accepted the imperial titles and powers after the Senate had conferred them (7.2, 10.5). Similarly, the other rebels, Verginius Rufus (6.3) and Clodius Macer (6.1-2, and his coins *RIC* I² pp. 188-96), proclaimed loyalty to the Senate; and even the legions of Upper Germany, when they rebelled against Galba at the beginning of 69, at first made the same protestation (22.4).

condemned Nero and expressed grief for the death of his most illustrious victims: Suet. *Galba* 10.1, 'he placed before him on the tribunal as many depictions as possible of men condemned and killed by Nero...and deplored the state of the times'. Cf. also the speech which Dio attributes to Vindex, LXIII 22.3-6 ('his most illustrious victims' is Perrin's translation).

his care: Plutarch uses the Greek equivalent for the special imperial quality, *Providentia*, often depicted and invoked on coins and inscriptions.

general: Plutarch again is non-technical, using the Greek equivalent for *praetor*; Suet. loc. cit. states, correctly, that he 'declared himself the *legatus* of the Senate and Roman People'.

3. Nero...affecting to despise Vindex: Suetonius (*Nero* 40.4) and Dio (LXIII 26.1-3) give the same story, with some variations in detail; cf. also 29.3.

having heard the news of Galba...upended the table: Suet. *Nero* 42.1 is different, 'he collapsed and lay for a long time in a faint, without voice and half-dead'.

4. the Senate declared Galba a public enemy:no other source reports this, but it is inherently likely. Later the Senate would declare Nero a public enemy (Suet. *Nero* 49.2, Dio LXIII 27.2b).

5. he would loot the Gauls: Suet. *Nero* 40.4, 'he received the news of the revolt in Gaul so calmly and unconcernedly that he even made people suspect he was glad of the opportunity of plundering these very rich provinces by right of war'; Dio LXII 26.3, 'he thought he had got an excuse for money-making and murders.'

the property of Galba: as a public enemy, Galba would have his property confiscated; on his wealth see 3.1.

6. order Galba's possessions to be sold: not mentioned by any other source, but an obvious step to take.

the sale of Nero's assets in Spain: Galba needed money to finance his rebellion (20.3); presumably, if any legal form was observed in this confiscation, Galba argued that Nero, as a tyrant, was a public enemy of all Romans: cf. the oath which the Romans believed that their ancestors swore after they had expelled Tarquin, the last king of Rome, 'that they would not allow anyone to be king in Rome' (Livy II 1.9). Nero's property in Spain presumably included the properties which had belonged to Seneca and to Lucan, who were both from Spain, and both forced to commit suicide for involvement in Piso's conspiracy in 65 (Tac. *A.* XV 60-3, 70).

6.1. Many were now defecting from Nero, and...declaring for Galba: only Otho, governor of Lusitania, and Aulus Caecina Alienus, quaestor in Baetica, are known (20.3, Tac. *H.* I 13, 53), but it is very likely that Ti. Julius Alexander, Prefect of Egypt, also declared his support very early, since on 6th July 68, less than a month after Nero's suicide, he published an edict in Galba's name to rectify abuses (Sherk no. 80; cf. Suet. *Galba* 10.4, 'a ship from Alexandria arrived laden with arms, without any pilot, mariner or passenger'). Among the 'anonymous' coins issued for Galba in the first two months of his rebellion are ones celebrating the 'concord of the provinces' (Sutherland, *RIC* I^2 p. 213 no. 119, cf. p. 204 no. 15, 'Concord of the Gallic and Spanish provinces'). Cf. also the inscription of a later proconsul of Africa, Q. Pomponius Rufus, who was 'Prefect of the seacoast of Nearer Spain and of Narbonese Gaul in the war which the commander [or "emperor"] Galba fought for the republic [or "the state"]' (McCrum and Woodhead, *Select Documents* *of the Principates of the Flavian Emperors* [Cambridge, 1961] no. 31).

Clodius Macer: the literary sources are uniformly hostile, as Plutarch here, and Tac. *H*. I 7, 'Macer, obviously bent on causing trouble'; 11, 'Africa and the legions in it...had lived to see the execution of Clodius Macer and were content with any kind of emperor after experiencing a lesser master'. L. Clodius Macer was commander (and therefore a senator and ex-praetor) of the legion *III Augusta*, which garrisoned the province Africa, and was stationed at Theveste. Macer, when he rebelled against Nero, issued coins which show that he did not claim to be emperor but called himself 'propraetor of Africa', and claimed he was minting by the Senate's authority. He called his legion '*liberatrix*', 'the liberator', and raised another, *I Macriana Liberatrix*. He probably gained control of Carthage, the provincial capital, and planned to attack Sicily. For the coins, see Sutherland, *RIC* I^2 pp. 188-96, and the detailed discussion by K.V. Hewitt, 'The coinage of L. Clodius Macer (AD 68)'. As a result of Macer's rebellion, there was a grain shortage in Rome, since Africa was one of the two chief sources of supply, Suet. *Nero* 45.1, edict of Ti. Julius Alexander (Sherk no. 80), line 4, Tac. *H*. I 73; cf. below, 13.4. For his death see 15.3 and note.

Verginius Rufus: the actions and motives of Verginius are one of the most debated problems of the revolt against Nero. L. Verginius Rufus was born in AD 14 or 15 in Italy north of the Po, somewhere close to Comum (Pliny *Ep.* II 1.8), perhaps Mediolanum (Milan), near where an inscription in his honour has been found (Sherk no. 79A, discussed below), into an equestrian family (Tac. *H*. I 52). He was consul in 63. In 67 Nero appointed him to the command of the legions of Upper Germany, with headquarters at Moguntiacum (Mainz), in succession to one of the Scribonii brothers, Proculus and Rufus, who had been the commanders on the Rhine until Nero summoned them to Greece and forced them to commit suicide (Dio LXIII 17). It was therefore his responsibility to quell any rebellion in southern or central Gaul, as Gaius Silius had done in a similar situation in AD 21 (Tac. *A*. III 43-6). When the news of Vindex' revolt reached him, he concentrated his own three legions, *IV Macedonica* and *XXII Primigenia*, stationed at Moguntiacum, and *XXI Rapax*, stationed at Vindonissa (Windisch, in modern Switzerland), with their auxiliaries, and also summoned detachments from the four legions of the army in Lower Germany and their auxiliaries (Tac. *H*. I 51, 53, IV 17). With these he advanced into Gaul, to confront Vindex, but was held up by the resistance of Vesontio (Besançon), the capital of the Sequani (Dio LXIII 24). Vindex with his forces hastened to the support of Vesontio, presumably from the siege of Lugdunum (Tac. *H*. I 65), but before open hostilities took place between his forces and Verginius' army, the two commanders met for a private colloquy (Dio loc. cit.). What they discussed, and what, if anything, they agreed on, obviously cannot be known, though Dio states that 'as was conjectured, they made an agreement against Nero'.

In any case, this parley with a rebel would have compromised Verginius in Nero's eyes, so he had probably already been offered the position of emperor by his troops (section 3 of this chapter), and his bailiff Pylades about now made the vow to Jupiter, 'for the safety and victory of L. Verginius Rufus' – using terms otherwise reserved for the emperor – which he fulfilled with the inscription which still survives (Sherk no. 79A). However, despite the agreement, the two armies came into conflict (Dio loc. cit., Plutarch, section 4), Vindex' forces were routed and allegedly 20,000 were slain (Plut. loc. cit., Tac. *H.* I 51, IV 57, Dio loc. cit.), and Vindex committed suicide (Plut., Dio locc. citt.). Verginius' men thereupon again urged their commander to be emperor, and even threatened to support Nero once again if he refused, but with difficulty he made them agree to leave the choice of emperor to the Senate and Roman People (Dio LXIII 25, Plut. section 5, and 10.3-4, *Otho* 18.5-6).

At some time, probably before Nero committed suicide, some or all of the legions from Illyricum which Nero had moved to north Italy sent delegations to Verginius to offer him support as emperor (Tac. *H.* I 9). Verginius was obviously a man of importance, and his actions caused problems almost at once. His army had put down Vindex and his supporters, who were the ones who had brought Galba into the rebellion against Nero; therefore, once the Senate had recognized Galba as emperor, Verginius' position, as the destroyer of Galba's allies, was very embarrassing. Not surprisingly, there were hostile rumours that, in spite of his refusals, he had really wanted to be emperor (Tac. *H.* I 8, 52, cf. II 7, III 62). The story that it was against his will that his army had attacked Vindex' levies was probably invented to exculpate him from responsibility for the destruction of Galba's allies; it is hard to see how he could have acquired and retained his great reputation among the soldiers (whom he only commanded for about a year) as well as among civilians and his own peers (Tac. *H.* I 8, 77, II 51, 68; Plut. *Otho* 1.3, 18.5-6, Dio LXVIII 2, Pliny *Ep.* II 1) if he had lost control of his army at a critical moment before the only battle which (as far as is known) it fought under his command. See further 10.5-7, *Otho* 1.3, 18.5-6; Murison, *Galba, Otho and Vitellius* 15-26.

5. Galba became extremely alarmed: cf. Suet. *Galba* 11.1, 'there came the death of Vindex, at which he was especially alarmed and came close to despairing of his life'. Obviously Galba's single veteran legion and one legion of recruits, with a few auxiliary forces (Suet. *Galba* 10.2), would be no match for the seven Rhine legions and their auxiliaries.

wrote to Verginius: not mentioned in any other source.

6. Clunia: cf. Suet. *Galba* 9.5, who says that, before Galba rebelled openly, he was encouraged by prophecies, including one found by the priest of Jupiter at Clunia in his temple; however, he does not mention Galba's retreat to Clunia after Vindex' death. Clunia, the modern Coruña del Conde, was the chief place of one of the juridical districts of Galba's province (Pliny, *NH* III 26, 27); it is situated in north-central Spain, on a tributary of the upper Douro. A fragmentary inscription from there may mention 'imperator Galba' (*CIL* II 2779). One of Galba's last issues of sesterces (*RIC* I^2 p. 254, nos. 469-73) shows on the reverse Hispania, standing before Galba who is seated on a marble throne, and apparently offering him the empire, with the legend around, *HISPANIA CLUNIA SUL(picia?)*; the precise meaning of this elaborate design has so far defied explanation, but it certainly refers to Galba's receiving at Clunia the news of his proclamation as emperor.

The excavations at Clunia (*Clunia* I, II) seem to have produced no new evidence for Galba's activity. For its suitability as a (defensive) base see Haley, 'Clunia, Galba and the events of 68-69', though his suggestion (p. 164) that Galba may have promoted Clunia to the rank of colonia had been rejected with good reasons, in *CIL* II p. 383, over a century before he made it.

he spent his time regretting what he had done...rather than doing what was needed: How long Galba remained at Clunia depends on the date of the battle of Vesontio, for which suggestions range from late April to early June 69 (this last is certainly too late); see Murison, *Galba, Otho and Vitellius* 21-6, who argues for a date about 12th May. Despite Plutarch's remark, it must have been during this time that Galba organized his new legion and auxiliaries, convened a quasi-senate, enrolled a bodyguard of Roman knights, and fortified the town (Suet. *Galba* 10.2-3, 5), and that most of the 'anonymous' coins were struck.

7.1. it was summer: Nero committed suicide in the early morning on 9th June 68 (Bradley, *Suetonius' Life of Nero* 292); reckoning inclusively, Galba received the news on 15th June.

Icelus: It is unknown why he was in Rome. Suet. *Nero* 49.4 says he was cast into chains at the outbreak of the revolt, released on Nero's death, and gave permission for Nero's body to be cremated. Nothing is known about his earlier life, though obviously he had already gained Galba's confidence, among other things, as one of his sexual partners (Suet. *Galba* 22). For his later influence and death, see section 6.

in seven days: Icelus no doubt went from Rome to Ostia, then by sea to Tarraco, and from there to Clunia by use of the official posting service. According to Pliny, *NH* XIX 4, the voyage from Tarraco to Ostia would take four days as a minimum; this, however, gives no usable information for voyages in the other direction (cf. Casson, *The Ancient Mariners* 234). The distance from Rome to Ostia is about 25km, which would take less than two hours for an official express messenger; Icelus presumably hired a fast vessel at the port – expense was no object – and was lucky with the winds. From Tarraco to Clunia is about 500km; a messenger brought the news of the rebellion of the two legions at Moguntiacum (22) to Vitellius at Colonia Agrippinensis, about 175km away, by the same night, even though it was mid-winter; Pliny *NH* VII 84 states that Tiberius, in 9 BC, covered 200 Roman miles (about 300km) in 24 hours, riding in a carriage, so a speed in summer of well over 200km per day must have been possible. Only Plutarch gives the details about Icelus' arrival; Suetonius mentions incidentally that he brought the first news (*Galba* 22.2), but in his systematic account (11.2) only says 'Galba learnt from messengers arriving from Rome that Nero was dead and all had sworn allegiance to himself'.

2. When Nero was still alive...first the army, then the Senate and people had proclaimed Galba emperor: cf. Suet. *Nero* 47.3-49.4 for a more detailed account, and the fragments of Dio LXII 27.2b-29.2. Both agree on the salient point that Nero was stripped of his imperial powers while still alive.

3. he had...seen Nero lying dead: cf. Suet. *Nero* 49.4, 'Icelus, Galba's freedman, gave permission for Nero's body to be cremated.'

4. However, two days later, Titus...one of the Praetorians, arrived: the manuscripts give the name either as 'Titus' or, even less usefully, as 'not Titus', and mark a gap after it. Editors have corrected 'not Titus' to 'Vinius Titus', which in Greek is fairly similar, and a possible order, but common sense indicates that this is very unlikely. Vinius was commander of the legion in Spain (4.7 and note), and would need the emperor's permission to leave not merely his post but his province. And when would he have travelled to Rome? According to Plutarch (4.7), it was he who had encouraged Galba to rebel; even if this could have been kept a secret, for the second most important man from the province Tarraconensis to arrive at Rome when his commander was a rebel must have aroused instant suspicion. Icelus, Galba's trusted freedman, was put into custody at the very beginning of the disturbances (Suet. *Galba* 49.4); one cannot imagine that Vinius would be treated more leniently. We cannot know who 'Titus' or 'not Titus' was; for details, and an improbable suggestion, see Kessissoglu, 'Plutarch V. Galbae 7, 5', (in German).

reported the decisions of the Senate in detail: presumably the actual wording of the Senate's decrees which deposed Nero and voted the imperial titles and powers to Galba. Strictly, they would still have to be ratified by the Roman People, but that was a formality. The last section of an inscription recording the vote of the imperial powers to Vespasian, some eighteen months later, survives (Sherk no. 82). It was presumably after this that Galba ended the minting of the 'anonymous' Republican-style coins and began to strike the 'horseman' coins, with the legend *Galba Imp(erator)*, but without a portrait: instead, the obverse shows him riding, in military dress; the reverses continue several of the themes of the 'anonymous' coinage (*RIC* I² p. 232 nos. 1-3, pp. 236-7 nos. 85-94; see also p. 257 nos. 516-8). These coins were struck outside Italy, in Spain and perhaps in Gaul.

6. He was promoted to a post of honour: the post, like the recipient, is unknown.

on Icelus Galba conferred the right to the gold ring: the right to wear a gold ring was reserved for *equites*, 'Roman knights'. An *eques* had to be of good character, free birth, have property worth a minimum of 400,000 sesterces (i.e. 100,000 *denarii*), and be entered on the list of 'knights' by the emperor. Icelus, as an ex-slave, obviously did not have the first prerequisite; however, by a fiction, called *restitutio natalium*, 'return of birth-right', that he had been born free and his apparent servitude was a mistake, he was made to qualify (see Crook, *Law and Life of Rome* 55, 63-4); the other requisites were of course no problem. Since he was no longer of slave origin, he also did not need to keep his slave name, which he had retained as a freedman – hence the adoption of 'Marcianus' (cf. Tac. *H*. I 13) as *cognomen* in place of Icelus. After Galba's murder, Icelus' enemies showed their opinion of the validity of all this by executing him in a manner proper for ex-slaves (Tac. *H*. I 46), i.e. probably by crucifixion.

he became the dominant force among the emperor's freedmen: cf. Tac. *H*. I 13, 'no less influential [than Vinius and the Praetorian Prefect Laco] was Galba's freedman Icelus', 33, 37, where Otho claims that in seven months Icelus had stolen more than was ever squandered by all Nero's freedmen; Suet. *Galba* 14.1-2 says the common name for the three was 'Galba's pedagogues'; also 20.6, below.

8.1. Nymphidius Sabinus usurped complete control: On Nymphidius see 2.1. Only Plutarch gives details of his behaviour during Galba's journey from Spain to Italy, and of his attempt to seize imperial power. Tacitus alludes to it, *H*. I 5, 'Already disaffected, they [the Praetorian Guard] were made still more restless by the unscrupulous intrigues of their Prefect, Nymphidius Sabinus, who was plotting to make himself emperor. It is true that Nymphidius was caught in the act and disposed of', cf. 25. Suet. *Galba* 11.2 and 16.3 does little more than mention the name; the fragments of Dio LXIV 2.3, 3.3, give even less detail.

seventy-three years old: on Galba's age, see 3.5 note; probably he was by now 72 (in his 73rd year).

be carried to Rome in a litter: Suet. *Galba* 11.2, 'he started on his journey clad in a general's cloak and with a dagger hanging from his neck before his chest'; Tac. *H.* I 6, 'Galba's march had been slow'.

2. extravagant reward: 2.2.

3. Tigellinus: 2.1.
give up his sword: the sword was the symbol of military power (cf. Dio LXVIII 16.1); to give it up meant resigning power.
sole commander, and for life: see note on the Praetorian Guard, 2.1.

4. These details of senatorial flattery for Nymphidius are unconfirmed, but not unlikely; after Tiberius left Rome, and Sejanus, the sole Praetorian Prefect, was left as his representative, between 26 and 31, the Senate and individual senators flattered him similarly (Tac. *A.* VI 8, Suet. *Tib.* 65, Dio LVIII 2.7, 4-6, etc.).
asked him to propose all their decrees: as an equestrian, Nymphidius was not a member of the Senate; presumably 'propose' means that he was to give his approval to the draft decree, and 'ratify' to give his assent after it was passed; even the emperors did not normally do this, though the Senate would not propose anything which an emperor might not approve of. See Talbert, *The Senate of Imperial Rome*.

5. the public slaves: there is no study in English on 'public slaves', i.e. slaves belonging to the Roman People, not to the emperor. W. Eder, *Servitus publica*, 167, states that this is the only evidence for public slaves being used by consuls.
sealed 'diplomas': for their use, and their restriction, see especially Pliny, *Ep.* X 45, and Trajan's reply X 46, with Sherwin-White's notes. They were permits to use the public post (see Suet. *Aug.* 49.3-50), validated by the emperor's seal, and valid only for the year in which they were issued. They also lost their validity at the emperor's death, Tac. *H.* II 54. They were supposed to be used only by travellers on official business: see Pliny X 120, and Trajan's reply, X 121, for an exception. Governors also could issue 'diplomas' in the emperor's name, presumably for use in their own province: a freedman of Vitellius accused Cluvius Rufus, governor in Spain, of issuing them without any mention of an emperor, as evidence of his intention to rebel, Tac. *H.* II 65. See *Oxford Classical Dictionary*[2], 'Postal service'.
fast changes of vehicle: the local authorities along the routes which the imperial messengers took were responsible for supplying the vehicles and draught animals: for details and references, see Suetonius and Sherwin-White locc. citt.
Nymphidius...his seal: since Galba was not in Rome, and presumably

had not sent any 'diplomas' with his seal there, the consuls must have validated the 'diplomas' with their own seals; Nymphidius apparently claimed they should have used his, thereby recognizing him as Galba's representative and plenipotentiary.

his soldiers: important messages were sent by *speculatores*, soldiers detached for special service, e.g. those who reported to Vitellius that the eastern provinces had sworn loyalty to him, Tac. *H.* II 73. The Praetorian Guard had its own body of *speculatores* (Suet. *Gaius* 44.2, *Galba* 18.1, *Otho* 5.2. Tac. *H.* I 27; Chilver, *Commentary* 86-7), and presumably it was these whom Nymphidius thought the consuls should have used; they would owe their primary loyalty to him.

6. gave serious thought: i.e. considered deposing them. Since the consuls nominally were the heads of the Roman state, this would have been an outrageous act of arbitrary power.

As a gesture to the crowd: both Tacitus (*H.* I 5) and Suetonius (*Nero* 57) agree that opinions in Rome at Nero's death were strongly divided, with some sections of the populace regretting it, and others rejoicing; it was of course only the second group who could show their feelings openly.

7. Spiculus: Nero had enriched him with the property of one of his victims, perhaps Corbulo (Suet. *Nero* 30.2 with Bradley's note), and called for him to help him to commit suicide (Suet. *Nero* 47.3). Even though both Suetonius and Plutarch call him a gladiator, he is probably the same as the 'Scipulus, commander of the camp' mentioned by John of Antioch (Dio Cassius LXIII 27.2b) as killed by the Praetorians when they abandoned Nero (John very possibly garbled what Dio had written), and the Scipulus mentioned as an officer (*decurio*) in Nero's German bodyguard on a tombstone from Rome (*ILS* 1730).

statues of Nero...being dragged away: similarly at the downfall of Sejanus in 31, and after the assassinations of Gaius Caligula and of Domitian, in 41 and in 96, their statues were pulled down and broken up (Dio LVIII 11.3, Juvenal X 58-64, Dio LIX 30.1a – but see LX 4.6, for a variant story on the removal of Gaius' images; Pliny *Panegyric* 52.4-5, Suet. *Dom.* 23.2, Dio LXVIII 1.1). Verginius Rufus' soldiers pulled down and destroyed Nero's statues in Gaul (Dio LXIII 25.1).

informer: on informers (*delatores*) cf. Tac. *A.* III 25 and 28, IV 30, and Domitian's statement (Suet. *Dom.* 9.3), 'A ruler who does not punish informers, incites them'. Nero, probably early in his reign, had reduced the scale of rewards for some informers (Suet. *Nero* 10.1), but especially after Piso's conspiracy in 65, informers had flourished.

Aponius: nothing else is known of him.

some of them completely innocent: compare the events after the cremation of Julius Caesar, 44 BC, when the enraged crowd tore to pieces the poet Helvius Cinna, mistaking him for the conspirator Cornelius Cinna (Plut. *Caesar* 68, *Brutus* 20.5-6).

8. Mauricus: Junius Mauricus. He was not opposed to the punishment of informers: early in 70 he asked Domitian, on his first appearance in the Senate as representative of his father, the new emperor Vespasian, to allow the Senate to learn from the imperial archives who had laid accusations against whom, and received a temporising reply (Tac. *H*. IV 40.4). He certainly reached the praetorship and perhaps the consulship in Domitian's reign, but was exiled by him in 93 (Pliny, *Ep*. III 11.3, cf. Tac. *Agr*. 45.1) – so if Plutarch wrote these Lives under the Flavians (see Introduction, p. 3), the *Galba* must have been completed by that year. He was restored by Nerva, after Domitian's assassination in 96, and was equally outspoken then (Pliny, *Ep*. IV 22.4-6).

9.1. Nymphidius: 2.1 and note.

2. Callistus: Callistus had belonged to a private citizen, who sold him, and he finally became the property of either Tiberius or Gaius Caligula (Seneca, *Epistulae* 47.9). Set free probably by Caligula, he was one of his most important freedmen, but joined the conspiracy to assassinate him, and perhaps schemed Claudius' accession to the throne (Jos. *Jewish Ant*. XIX 64, Suet. *Gaius* 56.1, Tac. *A*. XI 29, Dio LIX 19.6, 25.7-8, 29.1). He was one of the notorious trio of Claudius' freedmen (Tac. loc. cit. and XII 1-2, Pliny *NH* XXXIII 134, cf. XXXVI 60, Dio LX 30.6b). He died before Claudius (Dio LX 33.3a). Doubtless his influence helped Nymphidius' early career. Nothing is known about the seamstress and her daughter apart from this passage and the allusion in Tac. *A*. XV 72.

3. Martianus: otherwise unknown.

4. sole credit: see 2 and notes for Nymphidius' part in Nero's overthrow.
Sporus: Nero's favourite. After Nero's wife, Poppaea Sabina, died, Nero had him castrated because of his physical resemblance to Poppaea, gave him the name 'Sabina', and went through the full ceremonial of marriage with him in Greece (i.e. late in 66 or in 67), with Tigellinus (cf. 2.1 and note) acting as father of the 'bride' (Dio LXII 28.2-3, LXIII 13.1-2, cf. 22.4, Suet. *Nero* 28.1). He remained with Nero until Nero's death (Suet. 46.2, 48.1, 49.3, Dio LXIII 27.3, 29.2 [John of Antioch, probably garbled]). After Galba's murder, Otho took him as companion (Dio LXIV 8.3, not mentioned by any other source). Vitellius ordered him to appear on stage in the part of a girl

who was raped, but rather than obey he committed suicide (Dio LXV 10.1).

while the corpse was still burning: for Nero's cremation and burial see Suet. *Nero* 50. Despite this, the rumour soon spread that Nero was still alive: see Suet. *Nero* 57 with Bradley's notes, esp. pp. 294-5. For the belief, in Christian tradition, in Nero's second coming see Lactantius, *De Mortibus Persecutorum* 2, 7-9, with J. Moreau's notes, pp. 200-1, and Grant, *Nero, Emperor in Revolt*, 250-2.

5. men of senatorial rank and certain women: Plutarch mentions one of the men, Cingonius Varro, 14.7. None of the women can be identified, but for a woman who did play a part in the politics of 68 (Calvia Crispinilla) see Tac. *H*. I 73, cf. Dio LXIII 12.3-4.

Gellianus: otherwise unknown. For his return to Rome and report, see 13.1.

10.1. Verginius Rufus: see 6 and note.

4. one of the tribunes in his tent...told him to accept the empire or the steel: similarly, after Otho's suicide in 69, some of the soldiers attempted to force Verginius to accept proclamation as emperor, *Otho* 18, Tac. *H*. II 51. For the similar quandary of Germanicus in AD 14 see Tac. *A*. I 35. Josephus, *Jewish War* IV 603, tells the same story about Vespasian, who, however, gave way to his troops' demands and accepted proclamation as emperor.

5. Fabius Valens: Valens was one of the most important characters in the events of 68 and 69. For his career see Tacitus' epigrammatic obituary, *H*. III 62. Born into an equestrian family, he gained Nero's favour by acting in mimes at Nero's *Juvenalia* in 59 (see Tac. *A*. XIV 15) and thereafter, and became a senator. His promotion must have been fairly rapid: in 68 he must already have held the praetorship, since he was commander of the legion *I Germanica* at Bonn, in Lower Germany (Tac. *H*. I 57). He must have been sent with detachments from his legion to join Verginius Rufus, the commander in Upper Germany, when Vindex' rebellion broke out (see 6, and Tac. *H*. I 53). He was one of those who had tried to persuade Verginius to become emperor (Tac. *H*. I 52), and only after this failed did he persuade his men to swear allegiance to Galba, and proceeded to incriminate Verginius for his hesitation in accepting Galba's claim (Tac. loc. cit. and I 8, III 62). For his further career see 15.3, 22.10, *Otho* 6-7 and notes.

the decree of the Senate: voting the imperial powers and titles to Galba (7.2). Verginius had consistently maintained that it was the Senate alone which should decide how the empire should be ruled (6.3), and he accepted the decision once it was made.

with great difficulty: the troops in the Rhine armies were never reconciled to Galba, and he did nothing to win their loyalty. For the consequences see 18-19 and 22-3 and notes there.

6. Hordeonius Flaccus: an ex-consul (Tac. *H.* I 56), but the date of his (suffect) consulship is unknown. He was old and crippled in the feet (ibid. I 9), irresolute, and quite unable to control his men (ibid., cf. I 56, *Galba* 18.6-9, 22.7, and Tac. *H.* IV 18-19, 24 for his total failure in the Batavian revolt of 69). His mutinous troops killed him after Vespasian's victory (Tac. *H.* IV 36).

went to meet Galba: for Galba's recall of Verginius and his treatment of him, see Tac. *H.* I 8; Dio LXIII 29.5-6; cf. Pliny *Ep.* II 1.2.

Titus Vinius: see 4.7 and 12.

a life of calm and an old age of peace: Otho honoured Verginius with a second, suffect, consulship (Tac. *H.* I 77), which he held from 1st March 69, and he accompanied Otho on the campaign against Vitellius (Tac. II 49). After Otho's suicide, some of the soldiers again tried to persuade or compel him to accept proclamation as emperor, but he escaped from them (cf. note to section 4, and see *Otho* 18 and notes). After this, he is not heard of again until after Domitian's assassination, when Nerva gave him a third consulship, as his colleague, to open the year 97, and he died the same year, at the age of 83, and was honoured with a state funeral (Pliny *Ep.* II 1, cf. VI 10 and IX 19 for Verginius' tomb and epitaph; Dio LXVIII 2.4). The tone of Plutarch's account may suggest that Verginius was still alive when it was written.

11.1. The representatives of the Senate: who the members of this delegation were is unknown. For the choice of a delegation to Vespasian in the somewhat similar situation at the end of 69 see Tac. *H.* IV 6-8. It is remarkable that the Senate's delegation should have had to travel almost to the border of Spain to meet Galba; the distance it travelled from Rome is almost twice the distance Galba had to travel, from Clunia to Narbonne. For the likely date of the meeting, see Murison, *Galba, Otho and Vitellius* 28-9 (read 'Narbo' for 'Tarraco', top of p. 29).

Narbonne: the Roman Narbo, after which Gallia Narbonensis, the area of Gaul which the Romans controlled before Caesar's conquests, was named. Augustus made this area a separate 'senatorial' province in 22 BC, and the governor, always an ex-praetor, resided at Narbo. The town lies near the coast, in south-west Gaul, on the road to Spain. The Romans settled it as a colony about 114 BC, and Caesar established another colony there in 45 BC (Salmon, *Roman Colonization under the Republic* 121-3, 136); it was one of the most important ports and prosperous towns of Gaul (Diodorus V 38.5,

Strabo IV 1.12.186c).

his yearning people: not mere flattery – the population of Rome wished to keep the emperor in or near the city, since this would guarantee them his attention, and in particular ensure a plentiful supply of shows. Tiberius was unpopular largely because he stayed away from Rome for the last eleven years of his reign; Nero cancelled a trip to Egypt on the pretext that the populace wished him to remain in Rome (Tac. *A*. XV 36). Cf. Martial's plea to the Rhine to send the new emperor, Trajan, to Rome (X 7).

2. a full array of the imperial table-service…sent to him by Nymphidius: probably separately from, and more quickly than, the senatorial delegation.

…nothing but his own: Galba's restraint is depicted by our other sources, and even by Plutarch later (16.2), as ridiculous parsimony. No doubt, however, considering his wealth, his dining arrangements were adequate.

3. 'populism': the Greek word literally means 'demagoguery', i.e. pandering to the wishes of the populace.

4. puppet of Vinius: Tac. *H*. I 6 and 12 gives the same impression, while Suet. *Galba* 14.2 says the people called Vinius, along with Galba's freedman Icelus and his Praetorian Prefect Laco, Galba's three tutors (cf. note on 7.6).

12. For the details of Vinius' earlier career, see especially Tacitus' obituary, *H*. I 48, which gives the same details as Plutarch (except that in Tacitus the cup Vinius stole is golden, as it is in Suet *Claud*. 32, who does not mention Vinius' name), but adds his age at death – 47 years, which fixes his date of birth as 21 or perhaps 22 – his praetorship and legionary command (dates unknown, but under Claudius), and his proconsulship in Gallia Narbonensis (date unknown), which Tacitus praises as 'strict and honest'. Both Plutarch and Tacitus obviously derive from the 'Common Source', to which Tacitus probably added information and comments of his own, notably in his description of Vinius' character and ability. Neither author, unfortunately, explains how he came to be appointed legionary commander in Spain, which seems like a demotion after his proconsulship.

2. Calvisius Sabinus: consul 26, governor of Pannonia under Gaius (perhaps appointed by Tiberius) until 39, when he was recalled, and accused, probably of treason, together with his wife; they both committed suicide before the trial, Dio LIX 18.4. Dio, who does not mention Vinius, is the only source who gives the wife's name, Cornelia; it is possible she was the sister of Sabinus' colleague as consul, Cn. Cornelius Lentulus Gaetulicus, who also was put to death by Gaius in 39, Dio LIX 22.4. The sensational story about Vinius and Cornelia was probably part of the accusation against her and her husband, and Vinius' arrest and imprisonment only a minor act in the suppression of a much larger real or alleged plot.

13.1. Gellianus: 9.5.

Cornelius Laco: according to Suet. *Galba* 14.2, Galba promoted him from the post of *assessor*, or legal adviser (see Berger, *Encyclopedic Dictionary of Roman Law*, under '*Adsessores*'), to Praetorian Prefect. Obviously he was one of Galba's staff in his province; earlier, in Rome, he had associated with Rubellius Plautus, Tiberius' great-grandson (Tac. *H.* I 14), whom Nero banished in 60 and put to death in 62 (Tac. *A.* XIV 22, 57-9). Both Tac. *H.* I 24, 26, and Suet. *Galba* 14.2 condemn him for his arrogance, incompetence and sloth. He was one of Galba's three 'tutors' (7.6, 11.4). For his fate see 25.8, 26.1, 27.8.

of the Palace and of the Praetorian Guards: i.e. Praetorian Prefect. Normally there were two praetorian prefects; Nymphidius had forced Tigellinus to resign (8.3); presumably Galba had not actually dismissed Nymphidius, but by appointing Laco as his colleague he had frustrated his hopes of being sole prefect.

Vinius: 12 and notes.

2. manipulated by Vinius and Laco: this is the unanimous view of our sources; see the references in the notes to 12 and 13.1. Ironically, if Nymphidius' advice to dismiss them had been taken, Galba might have enjoyed a longer reign.

3. Tigellinus: 2.1 and notes.

his friends: 'friends' here is used in the technical sense of 'confidential advisers'. The prefects of the Guard and of Egypt (cf. Trajan's letter to Pliny, *Ep.* X 7) were among them, and they would include the leading senators, but the choice was left to the emperor's discretion (e.g. Suet. *Otho* 3.1, *Titus* 7.2). In general, see Crook, *Consilium principis.*

4. the city was dangerously unsettled: for a description of sentiment in Rome in the months after Nero's death, see Tac. *H.* I 4-5, 6.

Clodius Macer: 6.1 and notes.

the German legions: their dissatisfaction, ever since Vindex' rising, is a constant background theme; see especially chapters 6.4, 10, 22, and Tac. *H.* I 8-9.

the forces in Syria and Judaea: to suppress the Jewish revolt, four legions in Syria under C. Licinius Mucianus, and three in Palestine under T.

Flavius Vespasianus, the later emperor Vespasian (for details see Parker, *Roman Legions*, 138), in each case with commensurate auxiliary and naval forces. Tac. *H.* I 10, cf. II 1, indicates that Nymphidius' charges were as yet baseless.

5. Clodius Celsus: otherwise unknown. He may have been a Greek or Syrian from Antioch, the capital of Syria, or from one of the other Antiochs in the eastern provinces, whose family had been granted Roman citizenship, or from the Roman colony of Antioch by Pisidia, in southern Asia Minor, and so a descendant of Roman or Italian settlers.

a slum: the Greek word is the translation of the Latin *insula*, meaning one of the big apartment blocks of Rome which housed those of the urban poor who were housed at all (for a terse description of the life of a denizen of one such apartment see Juv. 3.190-211).

Caesar: already by the early first century AD, 'Caesar' had ceased to be primarily a proper name, and, especially in Greek, simply meant 'emperor'.

6. Mithridates: Mithridates VIII, appointed king of Bosporus (the modern Crimea) by Claudius in 41 (Dio LX 8.2). He later tried to secure full independence and, after various adventures, was surrendered to the Romans and brought to Italy in 49 (Tac. *A.* XII 15-21). Nothing is known of him between 49 and 68; very possibly the praetorian prefect was responsible for his custody, and that was how Nymphidius made his acquaintance. For his death see 15.1.

wrinkles and bald head: very well illustrated by Galba's coins. For the importance of physical appearance, see Tac. *H.* I 7, 'even Galba's age provoked sneers and disgust among the mob, accustomed to Nero's youth and comparing emperors, as crowds do, for their appearance and good looks.'

14.1. It was decided: Plutarch does not say by whom. The only evidence there is for the members of the conspiracy is the list of those whom Galba punished, of whom several may not have been implicated, and several of the guilty may have escaped; see 15.1. No other source describes Nymphidius' attempt to be proclaimed emperor, though Tacitus alludes to it several times, *H.* I 5, 25, 37; cf. Suet. *Galba* 11. The plot forms an interesting comparison with Otho's successful conspiracy a few months later.

the barracks: i.e. the praetorian camp; see note to 2.1.

2. tribune: each of the nine cohorts was commanded by a tribune.

Antonius Honoratus: not otherwise known. Apparently Galba did not reward even him for his loyalty; certainly he gave no reward to the rest of the Praetorians. It would seem that all the tribunes, and perhaps many of the men, had been informed of the plot, and would have supported it or at least not opposed it, if Honoratus had not taken the lead. Similarly, at least three praetorian tribunes, as well as one of the two prefects and several centurions, had been involved in Piso's plot against Nero in 65 (Tac. *A*. XV 49-50), and at least three tribunes and both prefects in the successful plot against Gaius in 41 (Jos. *Jewish Ant.* XIX 18, 37-8, 148, 191, Suet. *Gaius* 56, Dio LIX 25.8).

condemned them: how much of this speech actually represents Honoratus' own words, and how much was invented by Plutarch or his source, it is impossible to say, but in any case it represents what was said about Nero and Galba within a few years, at most, of the events described, and very possibly even at the time of them.

3. **Nero's crimes:** cf. Tac. *A*. XV 67, 'murderer of mother and wife, chariot-driver, actor, arsonist' (the praetorian tribune, Subrius Flavus, giving his reasons for joining Piso's conspiracy); Dio LXIII 22.2-6, 'ravager of the whole Roman world, destroyer of the flower of the Senate, defiler and killer of his mother, husband of Sporus and wife of Pythagoras, tragic actor, lyre player, singer and herald' (Vindex' reasons for rebelling). Obviously there was a fairly standard catalogue of Nero's crimes, of which the three which follow are an extract; it is satirised by Juvenal, with special reference to the matricide, VIII 213-23.

matricide: of Agrippina, daughter of Germanicus (Claudius' elder brother) and the elder Agrippina; Nero, son of Cn. Domitius Ahenobarbus, was her only child. Her death is fully described by Tacitus, *A*. XIV 1-11.

murdered his wife: Octavia, daughter of Claudius and Messalina, who was betrothed to Nero in 49 and married in 53 (Tac. *A*. XII 9, 58). Nero divorced her in 62, sent her into exile, and had her put to death, on 9th June (Tac. *A*. XIV 59-64, Suet. *Nero* 35.2, 57.1).

lyre-strumming or tragic acting: Tac. *A*. XIV 15; Suet. *Nero* 20.1, 22.3-24.1.

4. **believing Nymphidius' lie that...he had run away to Egypt:** 2.1.

5. **on Nero's tomb:** in fact, after Galba's murder, his head was thrown before the tomb of Patrobius, one of Nero's freedmen, whom Galba had executed (Tac. *H*. I 49; but contrast Plutarch 28.2-3).

Nymphidia's...Livia's...Agrippina's: i.e. Nymphidius (see 2.1 and notes), Galba, adopted by Livia Ocellina, his step-mother (Suet. *Galba* 3.4-4.1), who apparently was no relation to Livia, Augustus' wife (on Galba's relations with her, see 3.2 and notes), and Nero (see section 3 and notes).

avengers of Nero: cf. Tac. *H*. I 5, 'The soldiery in the city had long been indoctrinated with loyalty to the Caesars and was persuaded to desert Nero by cunning and surprise rather than by its own intention.'

7. as some say: this does not prove that Plutarch consulted several authorities; he may have taken this phrase from his source.

Cingonius Varro: he was already a senator in 61 (Tac. *A*. XIV 45), and was designated suffect consul for the end of 68 (Tac. *H*. I 6). For his death, see 15.1 and notes.

10. Septimius: otherwise unknown but presumably one of Nymphidius' bodyguard.

15.1. Cingonius: see 14.7. Tacitus also mentions his death (*H*. I 6, 37), indicating that he was executed before Galba reached Rome.

Mithridates: see 13.6 and notes.

neither lawful nor humane: Tacitus (perhaps also drawing on the 'Common Source') indicates that this was a widespread opinion, 'Galba's journey was slow, and stained with the blood of Cingonius Varro, consul-designate, and the ex-consul Petronius Turpilianus.... They perished without a hearing or a defence, so seemed to be innocent' (*H*. I 6); cf. the words he ascribes to Otho, rousing the Praetorians against Galba, *H*. I 37.

2. fine promises: after Tiberius, every reign began with promises of good government and an end to arbitrary punishments, e.g. Suet. *Gaius* 15.4, *Claud*. 11.1, *Nero* 10.1-2, Tac. *A*. XIII 4. Cf. the opening paragraph of the edict of Ti. Julius Alexander, at Galba's accession (Braund no. 600).

Petronius Turpilianus: Publius Petronius Turpilianus, consul 61, then governor of Britain (Tac. *A*. XIV 29, 39); granted triumphal ornaments in 65, for helping crush Piso's conspiracy (*A*. XV 72); Nero sent him to command troops against the rebels in Gaul in 68 (Dio LXIII 27.1a, where Zonaras has perhaps garbled Dio's account, saying that Petronius joined Galba's side); for some discussion of his actions, see Murison, *Galba, Otho and Vitellius* 24-5. See also 17.4 and Tac. *H*. I 6, 37.

3. Macer...by Trebonius: see chapter 6.1, and notes. Tacitus gives Trebonius' *cognomen* as Garutianus and his post as procurator, so he was an equestrian (*H*. I 7); he is otherwise unknown. In *H*. IV 49 he mentions a centurion, Papirius, as one of the killers. Cf. also Suet. *Galba* 11.

Fonteius: Fonteius Capito, perhaps consul in 67. He commanded the legions of Lower Germany in 68, presumably sent as successor to one of the two Scribonii brothers (see note on Verginius Rufus, 6.1). He sent detachments of his army, including a force, perhaps a whole legion, under Fabius Valens (see 10.5 and notes), to help Verginius Rufus suppress Vindex' rising (see 6.1 note). On his greed and lust, as well as his death, see Tac. *H*. I 7,

52. He had executed the Batavian chief Claudius Paullus, on a false charge of rebellion, and imprisoned his brother, Julius Civilis (later to lead the Gallic rising in 69), presumably at the beginning of Vindex' revolt, since he sent him to Nero for judgement (Tac. *H*. IV 13). According to Dio (LXIV 2.3), when an accused appealed to the emperor, Capito seated himself on a higher chair and told him, 'Now state your case to Caesar', and for this reason Galba had him put to death. Tacitus, however, says that the official story was that he was plotting rebellion against Galba, but that it was rumoured that Fabius Valens had tried to persuade him to revolt, and killed him when his persuasion failed (Tac. *H*. I 7, III 62). Despite his faults, he was popular with his troops, who later took vengeance on some of his killers (Tac. *H*. I 8, 58), but (oddly?) not on Valens, whom they always held in high regard. Tac. *H*. I 7 names both Valens and another legionary legate, Cornelius Aquinus, as responsible for his death. Suet. *Galba* 11 mentions the suppression of Nymphidius Sabinus, Fonteius Capito, and Clodius Macer, perhaps in the chronological order of their deaths.

Turpilianus...defenceless and unarmed: his troops (see note on section 2) must therefore have deserted him, or else he voluntarily joined Galba's side with his men.

5. five kilometres: the Greek is 'about 25 stades'; the stade was a common but rather variable measure of length, which, depending on the system, varied between about 175 and 195 metres; here it is probably one eighth of a Roman mile, or 185 metres. Tac. *H*. I 6 and Suet. *Galba* 12.2 both place this event at Galba's first entrance into Rome. There is no reason to question Plutarch's more precise and detailed account. See also Dio LXIV 3.1-2.

oarsmen: the Roman fleets were manned by subjects who were not Roman citizens, and their pay and conditions of service were significantly worse than those of the legionaries. Nero had enrolled a legion (later called *I Adiutrix*) from the naval personnel stationed at the two main bases, Misenum and Ravenna (Parker, *Roman Legions* 100), and the men were now understandably anxious to have their military rank, and their new status as Roman citizens, confirmed by Galba. Murison, *Commentary* 63, oddly denies that the men involved were the *I Adiutrix*, and suggests that they were the later *II Adiutrix*, which Nero would have started raising but whose organization was still incomplete.

6. standards: especially the legionary standard, the eagle, without which no legion was properly constituted, but also the standards for the cohorts and smaller units (cf. Tac. *H*. V 16, for the 'blooding' of new standards by *II Adiutrix*). Suet. *Galba* 12.2 uses almost the same expressions about the demand. In general on military standards, see Webster, *Roman Imperial Army* 133-9.

7. ordered his cavalry to charge: Galba had a long established reputation as a strict disciplinarian, ever since Gaius had appointed him in 39 to restore the discipline of the legions of Upper Germany (Suet. *Galba* 6.2-3).

8. a mess of blood and corpses: Tac. *H.* I 6, talks of 'thousands of unarmed men massacred' (which does not agree with Plutarch's 'some...even drew their swords'), and later, I 37, makes Otho state not only 'he slaughtered so many thousands of totally innocent soldiers', but 'before the eyes of the city he ordered the decimation of men whose surrender he had accepted, when they entrusted themselves to his mercy'; Suet. *Galba* 12.2, 'he not only scattered them with a cavalry charge, but actually decimated them'; Dio LXIV 3.2, 'about 7,000 were killed on the spot, the others were later decimated'. Since the total complement of a legion was 5,600 men, Dio's figure is obviously impossible, and Tacitus' statement also exaggerated: even if Nero had in fact started raising two legions from the fleets, and both were involved, it is hard to believe that nearly two-thirds of them (Dio's figure), or at least about one-third (Tacitus' 'thousands...massacred'), were killed by one cavalry charge. Decimation, if applied strictly to a full strength legion, would kill 560 men, quite enough to cause consternation and form the basis for later exaggeration. Probably several dozen of the protestors were killed by the cavalry, and one tenth of the survivors later suffered capital punishment.

However, on 22nd December Galba granted honourable discharge and Roman citizenship to men of the legion *I Adiutrix* who had served their time (*ILS* 1988) – obviously their years of naval service were included. Nonetheless, the legion never forgave him, and enthusiastically supported Otho, Tac. *H.* 1.31, 36, 87.

9. feeble old man...fear and apprehension: cf. Tac. *H.* I 7, 'Galba's very age was a reason to mock and despise him', Suet. *Galba* 12, 'his reputation for cruelty had preceded him from Spain', and Otho's speech to the Praetorians, Tac. *H.* I 37.

16.1. Nero's reckless extravagance: Suet. *Nero* 30, gives examples. Tac. *H.* I 20, says that Nero had given away 2,200 million sesterces.

seemed to go too far: for his reputation as miser, see Suet. *Galba* 12.1, 13.1, Tac. *H.* I 5, 18.

2. Canus: see much the same story in Suet. *Galba* 12.3, except that he makes the gift five *denarii*, which would be worth only one-fifth of one gold piece. Legionaries were paid the equivalent of nine gold pieces a year. Plutarch mentions a saying by Canus in *Moralia* 786C; Philostratus, *Life of*

Apollonius V 21, invents a 'philosophical' dialogue between him and Apollonius; and Martial mentions him twice, IV 5.8, X 3, as a famous and popular performer in Flavian Rome.

3. nine-tenths of the value of the gifts: Tac. *H.* I 20, gives their total as 2,200 million sesterces, but does not state who the recipients were; Suet. *Galba* 15.1 is not quite clear, saying that nine-tenths of the gifts were to be revoked, and that 'even if actors and athletes had sold anything given them, it should be taken from the purchasers'. Probably Plutarch is, once again, the most precise.

satyrs: by Plutarch's time, the stock representation of satyrs was as youths with goats' legs, tail and ears, companions of Dionysus, the god of wine, irrepressibly drunken and lecherous.

finding those: Suet. *Galba* 15.2 mentions a commission of fifty Roman knights; Tac. *H.* I 20, gives their number as thirty. We cannot know which is right.

4. the net spread wide: Tac. loc. cit. writes of 'auction sales and confiscators everywhere, the city in turmoil with law-suits'. The confiscations spread to the provinces, at least to Greece: Dio LXIII 14.12 mentions gifts by Nero of 250,000 *denarii* to judges at the Olympic Games, and of 100,000 to the Pythian priestess at Delphi, both of which Galba recovered.

Vinius envied and abhorred: on Vinius' avarice and wealth see esp. the speech Tacitus gives to Otho, *H.* I 37, also I 48; Suet. *Galba* 14.2.

5. Hesiod: *Works and Days* 362; the next line is 'in between be sparing; it is wretched to be sparing at the bottom'. Since Galba's life, and with it Vinius' chances of profit, was nearly gone, Vinius was using the little that remained without stint. Tac. *H.* I 7 makes the same point about Galba's slaves.

17.1. Vinius either thwarted or misrepresented: thus proving true Nymphidius' warning (13.2). Was Plutarch aware of the irony?

2. Helius, Polycleitus, Petinus and Patrobius: Helius had been left to administer Rome during Nero's visit to Greece in 66-7, with the power of life and death, Dio LXIII 12.1-3, who says, 'thus the Roman empire was enslaved to two emperors at once, Nero and Helius', cf. ibid. 18.2. Polycleitus was sent by Nero to Britain in 61, to settle the disturbances after the suppression of Boudicca's rebellion (Tac. *A.* XIV 39); during Nero's absence in Greece, he had plundered in Rome, Dio LXIII 12.3, cf. Tac. *H.* I 37 (Otho's speech to the Praetorians), II 95 (Vitellius' freedman). Patinus is otherwise unknown. Patrobius entertained the Armenian king Tiridates in 66 with a gladiatorial show at Puteoli, Dio LXIII 3. For the deaths of Helius, Patrobius and others, see Dio LXIV 3.4[1]. For the casting of Galba's head down at the site of Patrobius' execution, see 28.2-3, Suet. *Galba* 20.2, Tac. *H.* I 49 (who says it was at his tomb).

Tigellinus: see 2.1 and notes.

4. Turpilianus: see 15.2 and notes.

who made Nero deserve to die: echoed by Tac. *H.* I 72, 'he corrupted Nero to every crime…and finally deserted and betrayed him', very probably from the 'Common Source'.

5. they never stopped calling for his blood: Tac. loc. cit., 'they called for no one else's punishment more persistently'; then, under Otho, 'they gathered from all over the city to the palace and the forums,…then overflowed into the circus and the theatres, and clamoured with seditious cries', until the order was sent to Tigellinus to commit suicide. Cf. Dio LXIV 3.3, who claims Galba would have executed Tigellinus, had it not been for his unwillingness to seem to yield to popular pressure.

an edict from the emperor: cf. Suet. *Galba* 15.2, 'on behalf of Tigellinus he even denounced the people's savagery in an edict'.

terminal illness: cf. *Otho* 2.2.

6. Tigellinus and Vinius: cf. Tac. loc. cit., 'under Galba, Tigellinus was protected by Titus Vinius' power, who claimed that he had saved his daughter's life'.

widowed daughter: whom Tigellinus had allegedly protected, presumably after Galba's rebellion and Vinius' support for it was known, and before Nero's death. Her name was Crispina; her husband's name is unknown (Chilver, *Commentary* 69, suggests that Plutarch misunderstood the Latin word *vidua*, which can mean either 'widowed' or 'unmarried'; this seems unnecessary). Vinius had arranged that Otho would marry her if he became Galba's successor through Vinius' efforts, 21.1, cf. Tac. *H.* I 13. She buried her father's corpse after his death, 28.2, Tac. *H.* I 47.

18.1. the Gauls who had rebelled with Vindex: 4 and notes. The tribes and areas known to have supported Vindex are the Sequani, the Aedui, the city of Vienna (modern Vienne), and the Arverni (Tac. *H.* I 51, 65, IV 17).

2. remission of tribute and right of citizenship: cf. Tac. *H.* I 8, 51.

3. the troops: i.e. the Praetorians.

the full amount: 7,500 *denarii* (= 30,000 sesterces) for each of the Praetorians, and 1,250 (= 5,000 sesterces) for each legionary (2.2).

an utterance worthy of a great leader: the most widely reported of all Galba's sayings, Tac. *H.* I 5, Suet. *Galba* 16.1, Dio LXIV 3.3.

4. bitter and savage hatred: so too Suet. loc. cit., 'he was especially hated by the soldiers', cf. Tac. loc. cit.

5. a precedent for future emperors: cf. Suet. *Claud.* 10.4 (quoted in the note on 2.2).

7. the legions...under Flaccus in Germany: in Upper Germany; see 10.6 and note.

their battle against Vindex: see 4.3-5, 6.4 and notes. Also Tac. *H.* I 8, 'the armies of Germany...were disturbed and angry, through arrogance from their recent victory and fear they had supported the wrong side'; Suet. *Galba* 16.2. For their open mutiny, see 22 and notes.

9. as is customary among the Romans: cf. Suet. *Claud.* 7, *Domit.* 13.1 for favourable acclamations; the wording of the prayer is unknown.

'If he deserves it!': cf. Suet. *Aug.* 56.2, *Nero* 10.2 for emperors modestly qualifying requests for honours, or acceptance of them, with similar phrases.

19.1. From this point on, Tacitus' detailed parallel narrative begins (Tac. *H.* I 12).

the legions under Vitellius: the manuscripts have 'under Tigellinus', which is impossible, since Tigellinus had never commanded legions, and was now in retirement (17). Plutarch, after describing the attitude of the army in Upper Germany, is obviously now referring to their comrades in Lower Germany. They had no over-all commander in the period between the murder of Fonteius Capito (15.3) and the arrival of Vitellius, sent by Galba to replace him (cf. 22.7), at the end of November 68 (Tac. *H.* I 52).

letters were sent to Galba from his procurators: cf. Tac. *H.* I 12, 'letters of the procurator Pompeius Propinquus arrived from Belgica, with the news that the legions of Upper Germany had broken their oath of loyalty'; presumably these were the latest in a series of reports. For procurators see note on 4.1.

lacked authority not only because he was old but also because he was childless: Suet. *Galba* 17.1, 'thinking he was despised not so much for his age as for his childlessness'; cf. Tac. *H.* II 1, rumours that Galba might adopt Vespasian's son, Titus.

decided to adopt a young man...and name him his successor: adoption would only make the young man Galba's son, but would give him no public position, since the imperial power was not hereditary but was (nominally) conferred by the Senate, with confirmation by the People; so to make him his successor, Galba would also have to have him voted at least some of the imperial powers, titles and prerogatives. Plutarch is the only source to describe Galba as starting to think of choosing his successor on the news merely of disaffection in Germany; Tac. *H*. I 12 and Suet. *Galba* 17.1 make him decide and act only after the news came of the actual rebellion of 1st January 69.

2. Marcus Otho: Marcus Salvius Otho, born AD 32. There are four surviving accounts of his character, early career, and relations with both Nero and Poppaea, namely this one in Plutarch, Tac. *H*. I 13, Tac. *A*. XIII 45-6, and Suet. *Otho* 2-3, while Dio LXI 11.2 mentions their joint enjoyment of Poppaea. Though these accounts are mostly in close agreement, there are some significant differences; for a detailed discussion, see Murison, *Galba, Otho and Vitellius* 75-80.

corrupted him from childhood: Tac. *H*. I 13.

Paris 'the husband of Helen': *Iliad* III 329; Homer here and elsewhere uses Paris's more common alternative name, Alexander.

Poppaea: Poppaea Sabina, daughter of T. Ollius, who died AD 31 (so she must have been at least six years older than Nero, who was born at the end of 37, and one year older than Otho), and of Poppaea Sabina, one of the most beautiful women of her age, whom Messalina forced to commit suicide in 47 (Tac. *A*. XI 2, XIII 43, 45). It is not known why she took her mother's rather than her father's name, but her maternal ancestors were the more distinguished. Her first husband was Rufrius Crispinus, Praetorian Prefect under Claudius, and decorated with the insignia of a praetor and a consul by him, but removed from his post by Agrippina in 51 (Tac. *A*. XI 1, 4, XII 42, XVI 17), exiled by Nero after Piso's conspiracy in 65 (Tac. *A*. XV 71) and ordered to commit suicide in 66 (Tac. *A*. XVI 17). She had a son by him, whom Nero put to death (Suet. *Nero* 35.5).

3. his own wife: Octavia (see note on 14.3).

his mother: Agrippina. For her hostility to Poppaea, Tac. *A*. XIV 1.

4. gold and silver pipes: Nero apparently learnt from this, since his Golden House, built after the fire of Rome in 65, was similarly equipped (Suet. *Nero* 31.2), though the metal is not stated. Cf. Seneca, *Epp. Mor.* 90.15.

6. persuaded her to leave her husband: the date is unknown, but obviously a considerable time before Otho was sent as governor to Lusitania in 59 (for the date, see 20.1 note).

9. his own wife and sister: since Claudius adopted Nero, he was legally Octavia's brother, until Octavia was given in adoption into another family (which one is unknown) so that he could marry her (Dio LX 33.2^2).

20.1. Seneca: L. Annaeus Seneca, from Corduba (Cordoba), born 4 BC or somewhat later. Banished at the beginning of Claudius' reign for alleged adultery with the emperor's niece, Julia Livilla, but recalled by Agrippina's influence in 49 and made Nero's tutor (Tac. *A.* XII 8). He was suffect consul in 56, and, with Burrus the Praetorian Prefect, was practically regent of the empire from 54 until Burrus' death in 62, which was soon followed by his own retirement (Tac. *A.* XIV 52ff.). Nero ordered him to commit suicide after the detection of Piso's conspiracy, in which some of the conspirators plotted to make him emperor (Tac. *A.* XV 60-5).

praetor of Lusitania: Lusitania was one of the three 'Spanish' provinces, comprising most of modern Portugal and some of south-west Spain. It was normally governed by ex-praetors, appointed by the emperor as his deputies (*legati pro praetore*), so that it was anomalous to appoint Otho, who had only held a quaestorship, the lowest senatorial rank (Suet. *Otho* 3.2). The date at which he was sent is a problem: Suet. loc. cit. states that he governed the province for ten years; since he left it to join Galba soon after Galba's open rebellion on 3rd April 68, he would have been appointed in 58, and Tacitus seems to confirm this, by mentioning his appointment among the events of 58 (*A.* XIII 46); however, Suetonius also states that Otho feasted Nero and Agrippina on the evening before Nero arranged her murder (*Otho* 3.1), which was between 19th and 23rd March 59. Most likely Otho was sent in 59, Suetonius' 'ten years' is a round figure, and Tacitus included the mission to finish the story of the Otho-Poppaea-Nero triangle, without intending to imply a date.

2. neither unamiable nor oppressive: instead of this negative opinion, both Tac. *H.* I 13, *A.* XIII 46 and Suet. *Otho* 3.2 praise his moderation and integrity as governor.

exile: cf. the couplet quoted by Suet. *Otho* 3.2, 'You ask why Otho with pretended honour is in exile?/ He started committing adultery with his wife'.

3. the first...to join him: so too Tac. *H.* I 13, Suet. *Otho* 4.1.

to melt down for coinage: full discussion in Martin, *Die anonymen Münzen*; more briefly, Sutherland, *RIC* I^2 pp. 197-215, who is wrong in not ascribing all the anonymous coins (as far as they are genuine) to Galba.

4. in practical competence he was second to none: Tac. *H.* I 13.
in the same carriage: no other source mentions this.

5. ingratiated himself with Vinius: his good relations with Vinius are a feature also of Tacitus' account, *H.* I 13, 44, but he does not explain their origin.

friendly and approachable: Suet. *Otho* 4.2, 'He let slip no chance of doing anyone a favour'.

6. particularly obliging to the soldiers: cf. Tac. *H.* I 24 and Suet. *Otho* loc. cit., for an example.

Icelus: see 7 and notes.

Asiaticus: probably a mistake by Plutarch: Vitellius had a notorious freedman of this name (Tac. *H.* II 57, 95, Suet. *Vitell.* 12.1). Like Icelus, he was crucified after his master's death (Tac. *H.* IV 11).

7. a gold piece all round: cf. Tac. *H.* I 24, who states that a friend of Tigellinus, Maevius Pudens, actually paid out the money, and gives the value in sesterces, as 100 per man; Suet. *Otho* 4.2.

21.1. Vinius suggested Otho: Tac. *H.* I 13, who however mentions the intended marriage of Otho to Vinius' daughter only as a rumour.

3. not have made Otho sole heir: Tac. *H.* I 13, 'I believe he also thought of the state's interests; it was pointless taking it from Nero only to leave it to Otho'.

200 million sesterces: cf. Tac. *H.* I 21, 'extravagance even an emperor could not afford, penury unbearable even by a private citizen'; Suet. *Otho* 5.1.

postponed his decision: see note on 19.1.

4. appointed himself consul with Vinius as his colleague: cf. Tac. *H.* I 11, 'this was the state of Rome's affairs when Servius Galba (for the second time) and Titus Vinius opened the year as consuls'. Ever since Augustus, the emperor had appointed the consuls; the confirmation by the people was a mere formality.

expected he would announce his successor: in contrast, both Tac. *H.* I 12-14 and Suet. *Galba* 17 make the arrival of the news that the legions in Upper Germany had rebelled the catalyst for Galba's decision.

the military: here obviously the Praetorians only, not the legions.

22.1. the mutiny in Germany: it began on 1st January 69 at Moguntia-cum (Mainz), when the two legions stationed there, *IV Macedonica* and *XXII Primigenia*, refused to renew the oath of loyalty, tore the images of Galba from their place by the standards, and swore allegiance to the Roman Senate and People. For the background and a full account, see Tac. *H*. I 51-7. Suet. *Galba* 16.2 adds the interesting information that the legions sent a delegation to the Praetorians to say that they were dissatisfied with the emperor made in Spain, and the Praetorians should choose one whom all the armies would approve of. If this delegation was in fact sent, its mission was soon rendered futile by the rapid developments both along the Rhine and in Rome.

2. their donative: Nymphidius had promised, in Galba's name, not only 7,500 *denarii* to every Praetorian, but also 1,250 to every legionary (2.2). Cf. Suet. *Galba* 16.2, Dio LXIV 4.1 for the particular disaffection among the German legions.

two particular grievances: cf. Tac. *H*. I 8, 'the troops considered that the failure to send Verginius back, and his actually being put on trial, were an indictment of themselves'; ibid. 51, for the troops' anger at the rewards Galba had given to Vindex' Gallic supporters; 8, 53, 54 and 65 for punishment of his opponents; Suet. *Galba* 12.1.

state sacrifices: not mentioned by any other source.

4. Flaccus: Hordeonius Flaccus, see 10.6 and note.

traditional oath of loyalty: sworn on the first (the 'Kalends') of January since Tiberius' accession, Tac. *A*. I 8. Later the ceremony was transferred to the third, perhaps because of the bad precedent set now (Watson, *Roman Soldier* 49).

5ff. Plutarch's story is significantly different from Tacitus', who does not mention any such debate among the officers.

6. the very idea of submission to authority: so dismissing any notion of genuine loyalty to 'Senate and People'; cf. Tac. *H*. I 56, 'that oath seemed vacuous'.

7. one day's march: an optimistic estimate for a distance of about 175km, from Moguntiacum to Colonia Agrippinensis (Cologne), though a mounted messenger could manage it, section 9; Tac. *H*. I 56.

Vitellius: Aulus Vitellius; for details of his ancestry and life before his proclamation see Suet. *Vitell*. 1-7. His importance derived entirely from the eminence of his father Lucius, for whom see not only this passage and Suet. *Vitell*. 2.4-3.1, but also Tac. *A*. VI 32, 36, XI 3, XII 4-5, 42, *H*. I 9, III 66, 86; he was consul in 34, 43 and 47 (the first private citizen to be consul three times since M. Agrippa, Augustus' right-hand man and son-in-law, consul for the third time in 27 BC), and censor 47/8 as Claudius' colleague (the first censors since 22 BC); he died in 51. His son Aulus was consul in 48, proconsul of Africa, perhaps in 60/61, where he left a high reputation (Tac. *H*. II 97), and Galba sent him in October or November 68 to take command in Lower Germany, Tac. *H*. I 9, 52; Dio LXIV 4.2.

poverty: see Suet. *Vitell*. 7.2 for some (hostile) details, illustrating how 'some may sneer at it'; Tac. *H*. II 59, Dio LXV 5.

9. a standard-bearer: Tac. *H*. I 56 says he was from the fourth legion, and gives the same account in practically the same terms.

10. Fabius Valens: see 10.5 and notes. He was in command of the legion *I Germanica* at Bonna (Bonn), about 35km south of Colonia Agrippinensis on the road from Moguntiacum; the standard-bearer may have given him the news as he passed through. Cf. Tac. *H*. I 57.

11. Throughout the previous days: Tac. *H*. I 52 has Valens trying to persuade Vitellius to revolt from the time Vitellius arrived on the Rhine.

full of wine and mid-day food: Suet. *Vitell*. 8.1, has Vitellius dragged from his chamber in the evening, but he is probably misleadingly conflating, from the 'Common Source', the arrival of the standard-bearer late on the 1st, and the proclamation of Vitellius on the afternoon of the 2nd, after Valens' arrival.

'Germanicus'...'Caesar': Tac. *H*. I 62 and Suet. *Vitell*. 8.2 have the same account. Vitellius' official title was *Germanicus Imperator*. Cf. Tac. *H*. II 62. He finally took the title Caesar at the very end of his reign, Tac. *H*. III 58.

12. fine oaths of loyalty: Tac. *H*. I 57 for the phrase; cf. Suet. *Vitell*. 8.2.

23.1. Once Galba heard of the revolt: Tac. *H*. I 14, Dio LXIV 5.1.

2. Dolabella: no other source mentions him as a possible successor. He was in some way related to Galba (Tac. *H*. I 88), he had influence with Nero's German bodyguard, which Galba allegedly therefore disbanded (Suet. *Galba* 12.2), and he married Petronia, who earlier had been Vitellius' wife (Tac. *H*. II 64). Otho, as emperor, sent him into retirement at Aquinum (*Otho* 5.1, Tac. *H*. I 88); Vitellius had him put to death (Tac. *H*. II 64). His son was consul in 86, and therefore must have been at least sixteen in 69, so that adopting Dolabella would have fixed the succession for two generations ahead.

most of them Otho: especially Vinius 21.1.

Piso: L. Calpurnius Piso Frugi Licinianus, born in 38. For his parents see next note. Suet. *Galba* 17 says Galba had always held him in high regard and named him as heir in his will, on condition that he would take his name. He had long been in exile (presumably sent by Nero) until Galba recalled him in 68 (Tac. *H*. I 21, 38, 48). His wife was Verania Gemina, chapter 28, Tac. *H*. I 47. All the sources agree on his stern and puritanical character. Tac. *H*. I 14 says that he was said to be Cornelius Laco's (see 13.1) candidate. In general on Piso and his adoption, Murison, *Galba, Otho and Vitellius* 62-74.

Nero's victims, Crassus and Scribonia: Plutarch is wrong – Crassus and Scribonia were victims of Claudius. M. Licinius Crassus Frugi, consul 27, married Scribonia, who was related both to Augustus' first wife, Scribonia, and to Pompey the Great, as they proclaimed by the name of one of their sons, Pompeius Magnus. Pompeius married Antonia, Claudius' elder daughter, at the beginning of Claudius' reign, and was marked out as a possible heir to the empire, but in 46 he and his parents were all put to death, apparently for real or alleged conspiracy. For full details see Ehrhardt, 'Messalina and the Succession to Claudius', Levick, *Claudius* 58, 61. Their other children were M. Licinius Crassus Frugi, consul 64, killed near the end of Nero's reign; Crassus Scribonianus, killed at Mucianus' orders in 70; and Licinia Magna, known only from her tombstone.

went out to the praetorian camp: Tac. *H*. I 14-17 makes Galba first in the palace announce his intention to adopt Piso, and then deliberate where the official announcement should take place; Suet. *Galba* 17 also has the first announcement take place in the palace. Both agree on the formal announcement to the Praetorians, *H*. I 18, *Galba* 17. Tacitus gives the date, 10th January.

3. unmistakable portents: Tac. *H*. I 18, 'a day disfigured with rain storms, and extraordinary thunders and lightnings; traditionally this had been a reason for breaking off election meetings'; Suet. *Galba* 18.3 gives much less impressive omens.

he part read: Tac. *H*. I 18 says nothing about 'reading'; very possibly Plutarch misunderstood the Latin word *legere*, which can mean 'choose', as well as 'read', and which Tacitus uses in this sense here.

4. The soldiers...no donative: so too Tac., Suet. locc. citt.

5. Piso won the admiration: cf. Tac. *H*. I 17, similar remarks about Piso after the announcement in the palace.

6. fearing Piso, accusing Galba: more generally, Tac. *H*. I 21.

7. Chaldaeans: i.e. astrologers; the word had no necessary ethnic significance. For their influence, see Tac. *H*. I 22; in general, Cramer, *Astrology in Roman Law and Politics*.

Ptolemaeus: Tac. loc. cit. gives the same story; Suet. *Otho* 4.1, 6.1 wrongly calls him Seleucus, the name of Vespasian's court astrologer (Tac. *H*. II 78).

8. Tigellinus and Nymphidius: see 2.1, 9 and notes. No other source explicitly states that their former friends supported Otho, but Tacitus, *H*. I 24, mentions 'Maevius Pudens, one of Tigellinus' intimates' as helping Otho corrupt the Guard on Galba's journey to Rome.

24.1. Veturius and Barbius: the same story, with more detail, in Tac. *H*. I 25.

optio: deputy to a centurion, Watson, *Roman Soldier* 79; *tesserarius* is the next rank down, ibid. Plutarch's explanations, for his Greek-speaking audience, are too vague to be useful; 'observers' comes from the Latin *speculatores* (see note on 8.5), to which, as Tac. loc. cit. says, the two belonged.

2. Onomastus: Tac. *H*. I 25, 27 also mentions his part in the plot; cf. Suet. *Otho* 6.2. He is otherwise unknown.

3. to change the allegiance: cf. Tac. *H*. I 25, 'two common soldiers undertook to transfer the empire of the Roman people – and did so'.

sixth day: by inclusive reckoning. Cf. Suet. *Galba* 17.

eighteenth before the Kalends: i.e. 15th January, again by inclusive reckoning from February 1st, Tac. *H*. I 27. The Romans reckoned backwards from three fixed days in each month, the Kalends, the Nones and the Ides.

4. on the Palatine: Tac. loc. cit., 'before the temple of Apollo', which Augustus had built as part of his house on the Palatine. The close parallelism with Tacitus shows that both follow the 'Common Source' closely in their accounts of the sacrifice and its sequel. Suet. *Galba* 19.1, *Otho* 6.2 is similar but briefer, Dio LXIV 5.2-3 briefer still.

5. Umbricius: Tac. loc. cit. Pliny, *NH* X 19, cf. I 10, 11, gives his cognomen, Melior, and states that he was the most skilled *haruspex* (i.e. interpreter of omens) of his age. Presumably he knew of the plot (cf. Tac. *H*. I 26) and wanted a safe opportunity to warn Galba. Cf. Suet. *Galba* 19.1, Dio LXIV 5.3.

6. This was the signal: Tac. *H*. I 27, Suet. *Otho* 6.2.

7. 'house of Tiberius': part of the palace. For discussion of Otho's route, see Chilver, *Commentary* 88-9; Murison, *Commentary* 83.

'the golden pillar': the *miliarium aureum*, or 'golden milestone', set up by Augustus in 20 BC (Dio LIV 8.4), to mark the spot where 'all roads lead to Rome'; cf. Pliny *NH* III 66. It was by the temple of Saturn, and the *speculatores* in the plot were to meet him there, Tac., Suet. locc. citt.

25.1. Authorities: probably again from the 'Common Source'.
twenty-three: Tac. loc. cit., cf. Dio LXIV 5.3.

2. not as effete: Tac. *H.* I 22, Suet. *Otho* 12.1.

3. drew their swords: Tac. *H.* I 27, Suet. *Otho* 6.3.
ordered the bearers to pick it up: Suet. loc. cit. says that the bearers tired, Otho got out to run, stopped to retie his sandal, and was picked up and carried to the camp on the shoulders of his supporters. Tacitus gives no specific details.

4. an equal number came to meet him: Tac. loc. cit. makes the total number that joined the group on the way to the camp about equal to the original 23; Suet. loc. cit. has individuals joining the group as it went, but gives no estimate. Tacitus probably best represents the 'Common Source', which Plutarch has misunderstood.

5. The tribune Martialis: Tac. *H.* I 28, 'Julius Martialis'; Tacitus says many suspected him of complicity. He was later wounded when the Praetorians rushed into the palace, see *Otho* 3.10 note.

6. encircled by a preconcerted ring: Plutarch gives more details than the other sources, Tac. loc. cit., Suet. *Otho* 6.3, Dio LXIV 5.3-6.1.

7. the news reached Galba: see Murison, *Commentary* 82-3, for a discussion of the minimum time – at least one hour – it would take Otho to reach the praetorian camp, and the news reach Galba. The priest would scarcely have held the entrails for so long. But see Tac. *H.* I 29, 'Galba continued to entreat the gods of an empire he had already lost', which implies that the sacrifice was repeated, and the entrails inspected, several times. The conventional religiosity is probably Plutarch's own.

8. a motley mob: Tac. *H.* I 32, at a slightly later time 'all the common people were filling the palace, along with the slaves, and with discordant voices shouting for Otho's death and the destruction of the conspirators'.
Vinius, Laco: for these two and the imperial freedman favourite Icelus, see chapters 7.1, 12, 13.1 and notes.

Piso went to appeal to the Palace Guards: the cohort on duty at the palace, Tac. *H*. I 29.

Marius Celsus: A. Marius Celsus, legionary commander under Corbulo in 63 (Tac. *A*. XV 25), designated by Nero or Galba for a consulship in 69 (Tac. *H*. I 77), one of Galba's advisers on choosing a successor (Tac. *H*. I 14). Tacitus also praises his integrity (*H*. I 45, 71). See also 27.11-12, *Otho* 1.1-2, 5.5, 7.2-8.5, 13 and notes; Syme, *Tacitus* 682-3.

the Illyrian detachment: Tac. *H*. I 31, 'the picked men of the Illyrian army'. Nero had summoned detachments from the Danube frontier when Vindex' rebellion broke out, and they were still in Rome in January 69, Tac. *H*. I 6, cf. 26. For their rejection of Celsus and Galba, see Tac. *H*. I 31, 39. Plutarch omits the other attempts to rally military support in Rome, and their failure, which Tacitus mentions *H*. I 31; cf. also Suetonius' brief account, *Galba* 19.1.

portico of Vipsanius: Tac. *H*. I 31. The portico was begun by Agrippa, and named after his family name, but finished after his death (Dio LV 8.4); it was in the Campus Martius.

26.1. opposed by Vinius: Tac. *H*. I 32-3 also has Vinius urging Galba to remain inside the palace, and Laco and the freedman Icelus opposing this plan; according to him, Celsus had already been sent to the Illyrian troops. It is very possible that 'Celsus' is a mistake in Plutarch's text for 'Icelus'.

a persistent rumour: Tac. *H*. I 34, who also reports the belief that it was spread by Otho's supporters; Suet. *Galba* 19.2 states this as a fact.

2. Julius Atticus: Tac. *H*. I 35 calls him a *speculator* (see note on 8.5); cf. also Suet. *Galba* 19.2, Dio LXIV 6.2.

shouting he had killed the enemy of Caesar: Dio loc. cit. purports to give his words, 'Take courage, emperor, for I have killed Otho and there is no longer any danger for you'.

3. 'Who gave you the order?': all the sources mention Galba's question; only Plutarch gives Atticus' answer and the crowd's reaction.

got into his litter: according to Tac. *H*. I 35, Galba was already in his litter when Atticus arrived.

sacrifice to Jupiter: Dio LXIV 6.3, who says he set out for the Capitol, which is on the opposite side of the Forum from the Palatine; omitted by Suetonius and Tacitus.

4. the report…that Otho was master of the praetorian camp: Tac. *H*. I 36-8 describes how not only the Praetorians but also the 'naval legion'

(15.5) swore allegiance to Otho, and attributes a speech to him.

5. to go on, to go back: Tac. *H*. I 39, with slightly differing details.
his litter…: Tac. *H*. I 40 has a variation on the same metaphor.
first cavalry, then soldiers on foot: Tac. *H*. I 40 explicitly mentions only cavalry, but the course of his account makes it plain that infantry also were involved; Suet. *Galba* 19.2 has 'the cavalry who had been instructed to do the killing'; Dio LXIV 6.3, 'cavalry and infantry'.
the basilica of Paulus: only Plutarch has this detail. A basilica was a rectangular hall with colonnades which served as a centre of law and commerce. The basilica of Paulus (Basilica Aemilia) was on the north-east side of the Forum, first built in 179 BC, but several times repaired or rebuilt, most recently in AD 22 (Tac. *A*. III 72); for its magnificence see Pliny *NH* XXXVI 102.

6. ran to the basilicas and vantage points…scattering not in flight: cf. Tac. *H*. I 40, before the cavalry arrived 'all the basilicas and temples were full of people', then the cavalry 'scattered the crowd, trampled over the Senate'…and burst into the forum'. Plutarch probably copies the 'Common Source', Tacitus has adapted it for his purposes.

7. Atilius Vergilio: Tac. *H*. I 41 gives the name, which Plutarch's manuscripts have mangled, and says he was a standard-bearer. He is otherwise unknown.
the signal: Tac. loc. cit. Suet. *Galba* 19.2 only says that, at the sight of the emperor, the cavalry briefly halted, then rushed on and killed him.
pelted it with javelins: not in any other source.

8. no one defended him: so Tacitus and Suetonius; see next note.
Sempronius Densus: both Plutarch and Dio LXIV 6.4-5, make him defend Galba; Tac. *H*. I 43, in contrast, makes him defend Piso. It is unlikely that the 'Common Source' gave two variants, but it is quite possible that (despite Chilver, *Commentary* 101-2) both Plutarch and Dio made the same mistake independently, in remembering that Densus alone did his duty, and then wrongly supposing that he defended the main character of the story, instead of a subsidiary one. Plutarch gives much more detail than the other two sources. Densus is otherwise unknown. Plutarch's manuscripts again have a corrupt form of the name.

9. the vine-wood staff: *vitis* in Latin. For its use by centurions, and hatred by the men, see Tac. *A*. I 23. It is often depicted on centurions' tombstones, e.g. Webster, *Roman Imperial Army* Plate 1.

27.1. Lacus Curtius: originally a pond in the Forum, but it had been drained and surrounded by an enclosure centuries earlier, Ovid, *Fasti* VI 403-4, cf. Livy I 13.5, VII 6.1-6. Tac. *H.* I 41 has the same story of Galba's death with slightly less detail; Suet. *Galba* 20.2 mentions the place.

wearing a breastplate: according to Suet. *Galba* 19.1, he put on a linen corselet, though recognizing it would be 'little use against so many swords'; Tac. *H.* I 41, 'his chest was protected'.

'Do it': Tac. loc cit., 'his last words are variously recorded, depending on hatred for him, or admiration – some say he plaintively asked what he had done to deserve his misfortune, and begged a few days to pay the donative; the majority, that he offered his throat voluntarily, telling them to act and strike, if that was for the public good. The killers did not care what he said'. Suet. *Galba* 20.1 reports the same two versions, while Dio LXIV 6.5, writes 'he said only this, "What evil have I done?"' The 'Common Source' must have had both versions; Plutarch, consistently with his portrayal of Galba, recounts only the favourable one.

2. wounds in the arms and legs: since the breastplate protected his trunk, Tac. *H.* I 41.

Camurius: Tac. loc. cit, 'his killer's identity is not certain: some say it was Terentius, a serving veteran, others Lecanius; the most common story is that it was Camurius of the fifteenth legion'.

fifteenth legion: *XV Primigenia*, stationed at Vetera (Xanten) in Lower Germany; Nero had summoned detachments from there, Tac. *H.* I 6, 31, Suet. *Galba* 20.1.

3. Lecanius: So also Tacitus, but it should probably in both places be corrected to 'Laecanius'.

Fabius Fabullus: not mentioned elsewhere, though Suet. *Galba* 20.2 has a rather different story of a common soldier, returning from collecting provisions, cutting the head from the abandoned corpse and carrying it first in his tunic, then with his thumb thrust through the mouth, since it had no hair by which to grasp it. Tac. *H.* I 44, after describing Piso's death, says that the heads of both were set on lances and carried among the standards.

4. high priest and consul: Galba, like all the emperors, was *Pontifex Maximus*; he was consul in 33 and again in 69.

conscientious ruler: Plutarch's portrait of Galba is more favourable than that of our other sources, but cf. Tac. *H.* I 18, 49, Dio LXIV 2.1.

5. Sources assert: cf. Tac. *H.* I 44, 'it is said that Otho delighted more at Piso's death than any other's'; in both cases it is likely that the phrase derives from the 'Common Source'.

6. had been wounded: Tac. *H.* I 43.

by a certain Murcus: Tac. loc. cit. says Otho sent, with the specific mission of killing Piso, Sulpicius Florus from the British cohorts and Statius Murcus, a *speculator*, who dragged him from the temple of Vesta and killed him at its door.

7. Vinius: Tac. *H.* I 42, 'it is unclear whether immediate terror paralysed his voice, or if he cried out that it was not Otho's order that he should be killed'; Tacitus inclines to the opinion that he really was one of the plotters.

8. Laco: Tac. *H.* I 46 has a rather different story, that it was pretended Laco should be sent into exile, and he was killed by the soldier sent to convey him.

9. Archilochus: poet, soldier and adventurer, who lived in the 7th century BC. This is fragment 51 in Diehl's edition; it is known only from this quotation.

many who took part in the killing: Tac. *H.* I 44.

10. Vitellius hunted them down: Tac. loc. cit. tells the story in practically the same words and adds 'this was not in Galba's honour, but by the traditional practice of emperors, to provide protection for the present, vengeance for the future'; cf. Suet. *Vitell.* 10.1.

11. Marius Celsus: Tac. *H.* I 45; for him, see 25.8 and note.
the crowd: i.e. the soldiers, as Tacitus' version makes plain.

12. afraid to contradict: cf. Tac. loc. cit.
certain information: Tac. loc. cit has a slightly different version, that Otho pretended he was going to inflict greater punishment on him.

28.1. The Senate: since both consuls, Galba and Vinius, were dead, the next-ranking senator, the urban praetor, summoned the Senate and presided, Tac. *H.* I 47.

as though they were different senators: Tac. *H.* I 45 puts the same phrase a little earlier, to describe those who rushed to the praetorian camp to congratulate Otho.

the oath of loyalty: cf. Tac. *H.* I 47, Suet. *Otho* 7.1, and Murison, *Commentary* 109. For the oaths sworn to a new emperor, see Tac. *A.* I 7, at Tiberius' accession.

in their consular robes: i.e. Galba and Vinius, the consuls, not of course Piso and the other dead.

2. they sold Vinius' to his daughter: Tac. *H.* I 47, who gives no price; for the daughter, Crispina, see 17.6 and note.

Verania: Tac. loc. cit. adds Piso's brother, Scribonianus. Verania Gemina was daughter of Q. Veranius, consul 49. For her final illness, in Trajan's reign, see Pliny, *Ep.* II 20.1-5. She was buried with her husband, and their tombstone survives, *ILS* 240.

Patrobius: 17.2 and note; cf. Suet. *Galba* 20.2.

3. 'Sessorium': an area in the south-east of Rome, beyond the Esquiline, outside the 'Servian' wall, on the site of the present S. Croce in Gerusalemme; cf. Suet. *Claud.* 25.3, Tac. *A.* II 32. The name is found in the Anonymus Valesianus II 69, and introduced here for the impossible 'Sestertius'.

4. Helvidius Priscus: C. Helvidius Priscus, a Stoic hero and opponent of tyranny, son-in-law of Thrasea Paetus, one of Nero's most notorious victims; he was exiled by Nero and recalled by Galba, and was praetor in 70 (Tac. *H.* IV 4-6); exiled and later executed under Vespasian. Only Plutarch mentions his part in Galba's burial.

Argius: Tac. *H.* I 49; Suet. *Galba* 20.2 adds that the body was buried in Galba's gardens by the Aurelian Way.

29.1-5: with this obituary, compare Tacitus', *H.* I 49. Both obviously draw on the same source.

1. in birth and wealth: 3.1-2 and notes.

2. five emperors: Augustus, Tiberius, Gaius, Claudius, Nero.
more by virtue of this respect: cf. Tac. *H.* I 89, 'Nero was overthrown by messages and rumours rather than by arms'.
Some: Nymphidius Sabinus and Clodius Macer, 2.1, 6.1 and notes.
others: Verginius Rufus, 6.1 and note.

3. Vindex: 4.3 and note.

4. giving himself to its service: cf. Tac. *H.* I 15, who makes Galba say 'I was called to be emperor by the consensus of gods and men'.
Tigellinus and Nymphidius: 2.1 and notes.
Scipio, Camillus and Fabricius: typical examples of ancient Roman virtue. In chronological order they are M. Furius Camillus, conqueror of Veii in 396 BC, saviour of Rome from the Gauls in 390; C. Fabricius Luscinus, who as consul for the second time fought against Pyrrhus in 278 BC; and

either P. Cornelius Scipio Africanus, the conqueror of Hannibal in 202, or his homonymous grandson (by adoption), who destroyed Carthage in 146 BC. Plutarch was to write a *Life* of Camillus, which survives, and of one of the Scipios, which is lost, and to mention Fabricius' virtues in his *Life* of Pyrrhus 20-1.

5. Vinius, Laco and his freedmen: see 7.6, 11.4, 13.1 and notes.

The *Life* of Otho

The *Life* follows on immediately from the last chapter of *Galba*, without any introduction.

1.1. to the Capitol at dawn: 16th January 69, to sacrifice to Jupiter 'Best and Greatest'.

Marius Celsus: Tac. *H.* I 71, who does not make it plain that this happened on Otho's first morning as emperor. For Celsus, see *Galba* 25.8 and note.

no personal obligation: this implies that it was Nero, not Galba, who had designated Celsus to a consulship in 69.

3. In the Senate: only Plutarch expressly mentions this Senate meeting on 16th January, though it is implied by Tac. *H.* I 71.

Verginius Rufus: *Galba* 6.1 and note. Tac. *H.* I 77 says this honour was a concession to the army of Germany.

due to be consul: for designations Nero had made for the consulships in 69, and their alterations by Galba and Otho, see Tac. loc. cit., and Chilver, *Commentary* 140-1. Otho, as new emperor, took on the consulship immediately, with his brother Titianus as colleague, until the end of February (they replaced Galba and Vinius); Verginius was consul in March, with L. Pompeius Vopiscus; the remaining nine months of the year would be shared among the others already designated for consulships. Vitellius' victory in April of course changed these arrangements again.

4. honoured with priesthoods: Tac. loc. cit., with more detail. The four major priesthoods in the Roman state – pontificate, augurate, college of fifteen (*quindecimviri sacris faciundis*), and college of seven (*septemviri epulonum*) – were used as rewards, analogous to knighthoods and orders in British honours lists; their religious duties were ceremonial and not onerous. No private citizen belonged to more than one of the four; the emperor, and often his designated successor, were co-opted as extraordinary members into all four. For details see Ogilvie, *The Romans and Their Gods* 106-11.

exiled by Nero and recalled by Galba: Tac. *H.* I 77.

still unsold: so avoiding the unpopularity Galba incurred by trying to recover property which had already been sold, *Galba* 16.3-4 and note.

5. now their hopes rose: Tac. *H.* I 50 describes emotions at Rome after Otho's usurpation and the arrival of the news that the Rhine armies had proclaimed Vitellius, and, I 71, suggests that Otho's laudable actions were caused only by the emergency, and he was postponing his lusts and hiding his extravagance; Dio LXIV 7.3-8.1 also ascribes his actions to fear and the wish to make no more enemies.

2.1. Tigellinus: *Galba* 2.1 and note.

2. the city demanded: cf. *Galba* 17.5 for such demands under Galba; Tac. *H.* I 72, demands in the palace, the forums, and especially the circus and the theatres.

incurable physical diseases: cf. *Galba* 17.5.

incorrigible lust: Tac. *H.* I 72 says he committed suicide 'among the embraces and kisses of his concubines'.

3. Otho sent for him: Tac loc. cit. does not mention Otho's initiative explicitly, only that 'a message with the final demand arrived'.

Sinuessa: a coastal town of Latium, south-east of Rome, with therapeutic hot springs. Tacitus, our other source, says nothing of preparations for further flight.

4. a huge bribe to let him go: Tacitus implies that the messenger brought an order to commit suicide, not to come to Rome for trial; he agrees that Tigellinus cut his throat with a razor.

3.1. no trace of malice: Tac. *H.* I 47, 'whether he forgot past enmities or deferred them is unknown, because of the brevity of his reign'.

being addressed as Nero: Tac. *H.* I 78 and Suet. *Otho* 7.1 have the same story of the acclamations, and the reappearance of statues of Nero; for Otho's close association with Nero, see *Galba* 19.

2. Cluvius Rufus: see Introduction, pp. 3-4. He was appointed governor of Spain (probably of all three provinces) by Galba (Tac. *H.* I 8), so he could report that such 'letters of authority' (*diplomata*, see *Galba* 8.5 note) were sent to Spain; this does not prove that they were not sent to other provinces.

Nero's name: Suet. *Otho* 7.1, 'some say that he even added the *cognomen* Nero in his first diplomas and dispatches to certain governors'.

Romans of rank and influence: the same group as those mentioned in 1.5.

3. the mercenaries: i.e. the Praetorians. Plutarch, through his dislike for the Praetorians, equates them with the body-guards which classical Greek tyrants maintained, which were almost always composed of foreign mercenaries. In fact, however, Praetorians had to be Roman citizens and most of them were Italian.

wished him well: cf. Suet. loc. cit. 'he experienced the Praetorians' spirit and loyalty to him, which almost resulted in the destruction of the most distinguished order [i.e. the Senate]'.

4. Crispinus: Varius Crispinus, Tac. *H.* I 80, a praetorian tribune, otherwise unknown. For the Praetorians' riot, see Tac. *H.* I 80-5, whose account is very close to Plutarch's, even agreeing in verbal details, which must therefore come from the 'Common Source'; Suet. *Otho* 8.1-2; Dio LXIV 9.2-3; and Murison, *Galba, Otho and Vitellius* 120-30, who argues that it occurred on or soon after 3rd March 69. The details of what happened, and the reasons for them, are obscure, despite Tacitus' extensive account. Plutarch seems to assume the riot started in Ostia, but he has probably misunderstood his source; it would have taken several hours to cover the 25km from there to Rome. Both Tacitus and Suetonius clearly place the outbreak in the praetorian camp.

5. two centurions: only Plutarch gives the number; Tac. *H.* I 80 has 'the most conscientious of the centurions'.

6. eighty men: again, only Plutarch gives the number; Tac. *H.* I 81.

8. while he feared for his guests, they feared him: Tac. *H.* I 81 has the same phrase, more briefly. Plainly the 'Common Source' was capable of epigrams.

their wives: also in Tac. loc. cit.

9. the commanders: Otho had allowed the Guard to choose their own commanders after Laco's murder, and they had selected Plotius Firmus and Licinius Proculus (Tac. *H.* I 46), so might be expected to trust and obey them now. Tac. *H.* I 81 uses practically the same phrases.

10. forced their way: Tac. *H.* I 82 mentions that they wounded a tribune,

Julius Martialis (cf. *Galba* 25.5) and a commander of a legion who tried to stop them as they entered the palace and burst into the dining room.

12. twelve hundred and fifty denarii: for the value of this donative, see *Galba* 2.2 and note. Whether any other forces, besides the Praetorians, received a donative now is unknown. Tac. *H.* I 82 has the same amount (5,000 sesterces), and explains that it was announced and paid out by the Praetorian Prefects, and only then did Otho dare enter the camp. It seems this is the first donative he had paid, despite Galba's fate.

praised the majority: Tac. *H.* I 83-4 reports or invents Otho's speech on this occasion.

13. arrested only two: Tac. *H.* I 85.

4.1. others regarded them as ploys: similarly Tac. *H.* I 71, on the suspicion that Otho's new virtues were feigned; I 77, 'he did many things in haste, for immediate advantage'.

2. reliable reports: cf. Tac. *H.* I 50, 'a new report terrified the city, about Vitellius, which had been suppressed before Galba's murder'.

repeated defections: Tac. *H.* I 59, the Gallic provinces of Belgica and Lugdunensis join Vitellius, as do Britain and Raetia; I 70, a cavalry unit in North Italy, the *Ala Siliana*, declares for him; I 76, Spain, and Gallia Aquitania and Narbonensis, though at first recognizing Otho, defect to Vitellius.

Pannonia, Dalmatia and Moesia: the Balkan provinces; Tac. *H.* I 76.

3. Mucianus and Vespasian: T. Flavius Vespasianus, the final successful competitor in the 'year of the four emperors', and C. Licinius Mucianus, who was to encourage him to make the attempt; it is very likely that they had already begun planning, although Vespasian's actual revolt only began on 1st July, cf. section 9. They had been put in command of strong forces by Nero, to put down the Jewish rebellion. Tac. loc. cit. gives the same information, and adds that Egypt and Africa also declared for Otho.

4. he wrote to Vitellius: Tac. *H.* I 74, with the same story of an exchange of letters developing into mutual insults. In contrast, Suet. *Otho* 8.1 says he offered to share the empire with Vitellius and become his son-in-law; cf. Dio LXIV 10.1.

6. which of them was the more profligate: cf. Tac. *H.* I 50, 'the two who of all mortals were worst in debauchery, cowardice and extravagance';

Tacitus has probably moved this phrase from its context in the 'Common Source'.

7. Many portents and apparitions: Tac. *H*. I 86 has these two and more; Suet. *Otho* 8.3 a different one.

8. Victory mounted on her chariot: a statue-group given by Hiero, king of Syracuse, in 216 BC, Livy XXII 37.5, 12.

Gaius Caesar: i.e. Julius Caesar. Suet. *Vesp.* 5.7, 'when Galba was going to the elections for his second consulship, the statue of the deified Julius of its own accord turned to the east', as one of the omens that Vespasian would be emperor; this must have happened (or be alleged to have happened) late in 68. See next section, and Chilver, *Commentary* 154.

10. flooding of the Tiber: Tac. *H*. I 86, with similar but fuller details, including the subsequent famine, but no explicit mention of grain selling. Suet. *Otho* 8.3 claims that the flooding retarded Otho's march north.

5.1. Caecina: A. Caecina Alienus, see esp. 6.6, Tac. *H*. I 53, II 99-101. As quaestor in Baetica, he immediately joined Galba's rebellion, who put him in command of a legion, but then put him on trial for embezzling public funds. Presumably he was acquitted, since late in 68, though only an ex-quaestor, he was in command of a legion, probably *IV Macedonica*, in Upper Germany and joined the rebellion against Galba as soon as it began. Vitellius entrusted him with a large part of his forces to march into North Italy via the present Switzerland. For details, see Murison, *Galba, Otho and Vitellius* 84-6, 90-1. He deserted Vitellius later in 69, was honoured by Vespasian, but did not survive his reign. Vespasian's son Titus executed him for treason about AD 79 (Dio LXVI 16.3).

Valens: *Galba* 10.5 and notes.
already controlled the Alps: Tac. *H*. I 89, II 11.
Dolabella: *Galba* 23.2 and note.

2. Vitellius' brother Lucius: Tac. *H*. I 88 in very similar words.

3. Vitellius' wife and mother: Tac. *H*. I 75 'Vitellius wrote to Titianus, Otho's brother, threatening him and his son with destruction, if Vitellius' mother and children were not kept safe; both houses survived, under Otho perhaps through fear, but Vitellius as victor claimed the glory of clemency'; Tacitus does not mention the wife here. She was Galeria Fundana (Suet. *Vitell.* 6), by whom Vitellius had a son and a daughter; they joined him in Gaul after Otho's defeat (Dio LXV 1.2a, cf. Tac. *H*. II 59); the mother,

Sextilia (Suet. *Vitell.* 3.1, Tac. *H.* II 64) remained in Rome and greeted her son there when he arrived as emperor (Tac. *H.* II 89).

4. Flavius Sabinus: cf. Tac. *H.* I 46, as soon as Otho was emperor, the soldiers 'appointed Flavius Sabinus Prefect of the City, following Nero's judgement, under whom he had held the same post; many of them in this had regard for his brother, Vespasian'. For Sabinus' character see Tac. *H.* III 75; he was killed on the Capitol in December 69, after Vitellius' attempt to abdicate had failed. When Otho left Rome to oppose the Vitellian forces, he entrusted his brother Titianus with the security of the city (Tac. *H.* I 90), but soon summoned him to the north (7.6); Sabinus' son, a suffect consul in 69, also went with Otho (Tac. *H.* II 36, with Chilver's note).

5. Brixellum: Suet. *Otho* 9.1; contrast Tac. *H.* II 33, who makes Otho arrive there only after the battle *Ad Castores* (7, cf. 10.1). The latest discussion of the campaign is by Murison, *Galba, Otho and Vitellius* 91-100, 104-19.

Marius Celsus: *Galba* 25.8 and note.

Suetonius Paulinus: conquered Mauretania in 42; defeated Boudicca and saved Britain for the Romans in 61; consul for the second time 66 (the date of his first consulship is unknown, but it was probably early in Claudius' reign); 'no one had a higher reputation for military skill than he' (Tac. *H.* II 32). Tac. *H.* I 87 mentions Otho's appointment of him, Celsus and Gallus as commanders.

Gallus: Appius Annius Gallus, consul between 63 and 68; in 70 he was sent, with Petilius Cerealis, to put down the Gallic rising on the Rhine (Tac. *H.* IV 68, who calls him 'an outstanding leader').

Spurinna: T. Vestricius Spurinna, apparently not yet consul (Syme, *Tacitus* 634-5). He was 77 when Pliny wrote *Ep.* III 1.10, probably in 100 or 101 (Sherwin-White, *Commentary* 206), by which time he had had a distinguished political and military career, but nothing is known of him before 69. Tacitus does not mention him with the other generals in *H.* I 87, but in *H.* II 11 he appears as colleague of Annius Gallus. He may have been a source for Tacitus – whose acquaintance, Pliny, knew him well – or perhaps for the 'Common Source'.

6. insolence and insubordination: cf. e.g. Tac. *H.* II 18, 23, 39, 'the soldiery preferred discussing the generals' commands to obeying them'; and below, sections 8-10.

7. discipline was rather less than sound: cf. e.g. Tac. *H.* I 63-4, 67, before the invasion of Italy; II 26, 28-30, after arriving near their enemy.

arrogant for the same reason: i.e that they had made the emperor; cf.

Plutarch's opinion, *Galba* 1.6.

8. used to hardship: cf. the comparison the Pannonian legions made of their conditions of service with the Praetorians', in the mutiny of AD 14, Tac. *A. I* 17, 'they were not criticising sentry-duty in Rome; but they themselves were placed among savages, and saw the foe from their tents'.

Otho's troops: this applies to the Praetorians, not to the forces which Nero and Galba had summoned from the provinces. Cf. 6.2.

the theatre and public shows: Tac. *H.* II 21 uses very similar phrases at a later point in the narrative.

scorned routine duties: cf. Tac. *H.* II 19, who weaves into his narrative details which Plutarch generalizes.

9. Spurinna tried to force them: as Tac. *H.* II 18 makes plain, Spurinna was not trying to force his men to routine duties (that comes in Tacitus' next chapter), but to prevent them from clashing with Caecina's much superior force; Plutarch here is compressing the 'Common Source'.

saboteur of Caesar's interests: Tac. loc cit.

10. demanded a travel allowance: not in any other source; it is not clear where Plutarch supposed Otho to be at this moment.

6.1. derision: cf. Tac. *H.* II 21.

Piacenza: Placentia, founded as a Latin colony 218 BC, on the south bank of the Padus (Po); like all Italy south of the Padus, it received Roman citizenship in 90 BC.

2. Vitellius' forces: under Caecina (section 5). Tacitus' account of the Vitellian attack on Placentia, *H.* II 20-2, is different and more detailed; cf. Chilver, *Commentary* 184.

Pythian and Olympic games: the great Greek festivals at which Nero had competed in 66 and 67; he was accompanied by a Praetorian detachment, cf. Suet. *Nero* 22.3-24; Dio LXIII 8.3-4, 10.1-2.

3. fell on their knees before Spurinna: Tac. *H.* II 19 places their change of mind in a different context, with different reasons: Spurinna had led them out on a route march and ordered them to fortify a camp at the end of the day; the unaccustomed toil made them realize the danger they would be in if Caecina attacked them in the open, and they agreed that Spurinna's original plan, to remain within the protection of Placentia, was best, and allowed him to lead them back. This seems a more plausible story.

4. a fierce battle for the wall: Tac. *H.* II 22, with more detail.

most flourishing in Italy: cf. Tac. *H.* II 21, the destruction in the fighting of the city's amphitheatre, 'a most beautiful building;…no other in Italy was as large'.

6. Caecina: 5.1 and note.

Gallic trousers: Romans always found Gallic breeches (*bracae*) ridiculous, cf. e.g. the couplet mocking Julius Caesar, 'Caesar led the Gauls in triumph, then into the Senate-house;/there the Gauls pulled off their breeches, dressed themselves as senators' (Suet. *Julius* 80.2); Tac. *H.* II 20, describing Caecina, says he wore 'breeches, a barbaric garment' when he addressed civilians wearing togas.

his wife: Tac. loc. cit. gives her name, Salonina; she is otherwise unknown. Tacitus does not mention the cavalry escort.

7. Fabius Valens: see *Galba* 10.5 and notes. Tac. *H.* I 66 describes his avarice.

arrived too late: the parallel passage in Tac. *H.* II 30 indicates that the 'first battle' is not the attack on Placentia but the battle *Ad Castores* described in the next chapter.

8. eagerness to claim the victory: Tac. *H.* II 24, 'Fabius Valens was approaching, so, in order not to let him have all the success in this war, Caecina hastened to recover his glory, with eagerness rather than intelligence', and set the failed ambush *Ad Castores*.

7.1. Cremona: Tac. *H.* II 22. Cremona is about 28km from Placentia, on the other side of the Padus; it was founded at the same time. See Tac. *H.* III 34 for a brief sketch of its history.

Annius Gallus: 5.5 and note. See Tac. *H.* II 23, with more details.

heard: Spurinna sent him a dispatch, Tac. loc. cit.

that Cremona was in danger: Plutarch has misunderstood the 'Common Source'; it is plain from Tac. *H.* II 17 and 23 that Caecina's men had already occupied Cremona; cf. Chilver, *Commentary* 182.

his army: the new legion *I Adiutrix* (or at least most of it), two praetorian cohorts and some cavalry, Murison, *Galba, Otho and Vitellius* 105.

the other generals: Celsus and Paulinus, sections 3 and 4.

2. in ambush: Tac. *H.* II 24-6 gives a fuller account, often with the same expressions; the place was *Ad Castores* (= 'at the shrine of Castor and Pollux'), twelve Roman miles (18km) from Cremona, Tac. *H.* II 24.

Deserters: Tac. loc cit. only has 'this was reported to the Othonian leaders' (but cf. ib. 34, on deserters), and that then Celsus took command of the cavalry, Paulinus of the infantry for the coming battle. For a discussion of the battle, see Murison, *Galba, Otho and Vitellius* 107-10.

5. outright treachery: not in Tacitus, who only says that Paulinus was criticized by his men (II 26); but cf. chapter 9.4-5.

6. Titianus: L. Salvius Otho Titianus, elder brother of the emperor, consul in 52, proconsul of the province of Asia in 63, where Agricola, Tacitus' father-in-law, was his quaestor (Tac. *Agr.* 6.2). Otho had left him in charge of Rome, 5.4 note. For the date when Otho summoned him, see Tac. *H.* II 23 with Chilver's note, and Murison, op. cit. 106-7.

Proculus: Licinius Proculus, chosen by the Praetorians as their prefect (with Plotius Firmus) immediately after the murder of Galba (Tac. *H.* I 46); his earlier career is unknown. For his character, ibid. 87, II 33.

7. empty titles: Tac. *H.* II 39 says 'with the empty title of leaders'.

8. those under Valens' command: they were now at Ticinum (Pavia), about 75km from Cremona, Tac. *H.* II 30, who continues 'when the news of Caecina's defeat arrived, they nearly began another mutiny, claiming it was through Valens' trickery and delays that they had missed the battle'.

9. determined to stone him: Tac. *H.* II 29 puts this earlier, in a mutiny provoked by the Batavian cohorts; we cannot be sure which author preserves the 'Common Source's' context.

joined forces with Caecina: they reached Cremona in one march, Tac. *H.* II 30.

8.1. Bedriacum: the spelling in the sources varies between Bedriacum, Betriacum and Bebriacum; the first has been generally adopted by modern writers. The precise location is disputed (see Murison, *Galba, Otho and Vitellius* Map 3); the actual battle was not fought there, but close to Cremona. The strategic discussion took place on about 10th April (Murison 106-7). Tac. *H.* II 31-3 gives a similar but fuller account, but does not mention Proculus' and Titianus' arguments, which must have been in the 'Common Source'.

2. Vitellius himself to arrive: for his forces see Tac. *H.* I 61 and II 69, Murison 85-6; for his slow progress, Tac. *H.* II 57. Cf. Suet. *Otho* 9.1.

3. Paulinus: Tac. *H.* II 32, with more details, several of which (such as hints of the danger of a revolt in Gaul) seem to be Tacitus' additions.

Moesia and Pannonia: 4.2 above. The legions were *VII Gemina* and *XIII Gemina* in Pannonia, and *III Gallica*, *VII Claudia* and *VIII Augusta* in Moesia; the exact position of *XIV Gemina* is unknown; *XI Claudia* was stationed in Dalmatia (mentioned by Tacitus, and probably in the 'Common Source').

5. problems of supply: Tac *H*. II 32 elaborates, perhaps not convincingly; however, Plutarch says nothing about the further point in Tacitus, that the Vitellian army would soon begin to suffer from the unaccustomed heat. Cf. Suet. *Otho* 9.1.

Marius Celsus: *Galba* 25.8 and note.

6. fall from his horse: Tac. *H*. II 33, it had happened a few days earlier.

urging him to fight: Tac. loc. cit. and Suet. *Otho* 9.1 both make Otho himself impatient to fight.

9.1. various authorities give various reasons: none of this is in Tacitus, who only gives vacuous emotional appeals from Titianus and Proculus, but it may well derive from the 'Common Source'.

their impatience to fight: Suet. loc. cit.

2. no longer stand the uncertainty: Tac. *H*. II 40. 'Otho ordered the matter to be brought to a decision; he was sick with the delay and could not bear suspense'; Suet. loc. cit.

3. Secundus: see Introduction pp. 3-4.

4. movements towards reconciliation: Tac. *H*. II 37 for the whole story of a rumour that the armies would refuse to fight, and would try to find a better emperor; Tacitus expresses strong disbelief.

5. Marius and Sulla: Sulla took Rome (the first Roman to do so) in 88 BC; Cinna and Marius took it in 87 after Sulla had left for Greece; in the bitter civil war of 83-82 Sulla was victorious over his opponents, whose figure-head was Marius' son (Marius had died in 86).

Caesar and Pompey: the civil war begun by Caesar crossing the Rubicon in 49 BC and continuing, after Pompey's defeat and death in 48, until the defeat of Pompey's sons in 45. Tac. *H*. II 38 uses the same examples, and adds that of Philippi (42 BC), but turns them to a different purpose. It is clear that Plutarch is much closer to the account in the 'Common Source'.

drunken gluttony: Tac. *H*. II 31, 'Vitellius disgraced himself with his belly and gullet; Otho with his extravagance, cruelty and daring seemed more destructive for the state'.

6. Celsus: Tac. *H.* II 37 does not mention Celsus, but suggests that Paulinus may have hoped to be made emperor himself.

10.1. returned to Brixellum: Tac. *H.* II 39, Suet. *Otho* 9.1. For Otho's movements, see Murison, *Galba, Otho and Vitellius* 106-7.
   second mistake: Tac. *H.* II 33, with the same reasons.
   toughest and keenest cavalry and infantry: Tac. loc. cit., 'a strong force of the praetorian cohorts and *speculatores* and of the cavalry went with him'; for an estimate of numbers, Murison, *Galba, Otho and Vitellius* 134.

2. combat on the Po: Plutarch has omitted the earlier fighting by the river, Tac. *H.* II 23. Tac. *H.* II 34-6 describes this fighting rather differently.
   tried to bridge: Tac. loc. cit. states this was a feint; Murison, op. cit. 114-15, suggests this was a serious attempt to outflank the Othonians and open the way for the Vitellian forces to march on Rome.

3. loaded their boats with pine: to be fire-boats against the Vitellian pontoon bridge (Tac. loc. cit.); Tacitus omits this attempt, but cf. II 34, blazing torches hurled from a tower on the bank.

5. the Germans attacked Otho's gladiators: for the gladiators, Tac. *H.* II 11. Tac. II 35 makes it plain that the Germans reached the island first, and the gladiators from their boats tried to dislodge them. The Germans were no doubt Batavians (from the present Netherlands), famed for their swimming ability, Tac. *H.* II 17, 43.

11.1. an angry passion: cf. 9.1, Tac. *H.* II 39.
   Proculus: 7.6 and note. Tac. loc. cit. describes Proculus' incompetence in the same phrases.

2. at least twenty kilometres: '100 stades' in the Greek, cf. *Galba* 15.5. There are real difficulties in reconciling this with Tacitus' account, *H.* II 40, and the present topography of the area near Cremona. Murison, *Galba, Otho and Vitellius* 116-18, and Maps 3 and 4, suggests a solution. Plutarch had visited the battlefield in the company of Mestrius Florus (14.2), so his version of the account in the 'Common Source' should be preferred.
   Paulinus objected: Tac. *H.* II 40 adds Celsus.

3. 'Numidians': Tac. loc. cit., 'a swift Numidian on a horse'; cf. Chilver's note.

4. alarmed Caecina: Tac. *H.* II 41. Plutarch does not include Tacitus' story that two praetorian tribunes had just arrived from Otho's army to parley with Caecina when he received the news of the Othonian advance; this possible treachery would have fitted well into Plutarch's account, so it is likely that Tacitus had it from somewhere else than the 'Common Source'.

went to the camp: outside Cremona, cf. Tac. *H.* III 26.

5. the pass-word issued by Valens: Tac. *H.* II 41, in very similar words.

cavalry was sent out: Tac. *H.* II 41, cf. III 2, says that the Othonian cavalry drove them back.

12.1. For some reason a rumour surfaced: Tac. *H.* II 42 says it was rumoured that Vitellius' army had deserted, and 'it is unclear whether this rumour was spread by Vitellian scouts or had arisen among the Othonians either by treachery or by chance'. He goes on to describe the results in very similar phrases to Plutarch's. Suetonius, *Otho* 9.2, has no doubt that Otho 'was defeated by treachery; there had been expectation of a conference, the men were led out as if to agree to peace terms, then quite unexpectedly, as the two sides greeted each other, they had to fight', but his father had fought on Otho's side (10.1).

3. there was no system, etc.: Tac. loc. cit. describes the confusion of the battle more vividly, but obviously from the same source.

4. 'Spoiler': *XXI Rapax*, raised under Augustus, perhaps in 16 BC (Parker, *Roman Legions* 89), and stationed since Claudius' reign in Upper Germany at Vindonissa (Windisch, in Switzerland); cf. Tac. *H.* I 61.

'Support': *I Adiutrix*, raised by Nero from sailors of the fleet; see *Galba* 15.5-9 and notes.

wide, treeless plain: Tac. *H.* II 43, 'between the Padus and the road in an open plain'; he and Plutarch share many phrases, from the 'Common Source'.

6. Orfidius: Tac. loc. cit., 'Orfidius Benignus'; the details of his career are unknown. He was buried with full honours, ibid. 45.

7. the gladiators: last heard of south of the Padus, 10.5, which they tried to cross in boats, Tac. *H.* II 43.

Alfenus Varus: Alfenus Varus, camp commander (*praefectus castrorum*) under Valens (Tac. *H*. II 29); Vitellius later appointed him praetorian prefect, Tac. *H*. III 36. His earlier career is unknown.

Batavians: see 10.5 and note.

8. took flight towards the river: according to Tacitus, *H*. II 43, the Batavians routed and killed the gladiators at the river bank, as they were trying to land; presumably Plutarch has misunderstood the 'Common Source'.

9. Most shameful: in contrast, Tac. *H*. II 44 says that, after the battle, 'though the rest were broken in spirit, the Praetorians raged, claiming they had not been defeated by courage, but by treachery', and during the battle, ibid. 42, 'the Othonians took up the battle fiercely', with no suggestion that any fled without fighting. It may well be that Plutarch's strong dislike for the Praetorians has here controlled his writing.

10. many of Otho's troops gained the upper hand: not mentioned by Tacitus.

back to the camp: at Bedriacum, Tac. *H*. II 44, who describes the carnage in the flight.

13.1. Proculus and Paulinus: Tac. loc. cit.

fastening the blame on their commanders: Tac. loc. cit., in a slightly different context, 'each one blaming others for their own fault, as is the habit of mobs'.

2. Annius Gallus: see 5.5, 8.6 and notes; Tac. loc. cit. only has him calming the tumult and preventing the soldiers from attacking their officers.

Marius Celsus: see *Galba* 25.8 and note. Tacitus mentions his return to the camp, but does not mention this speech, which has the marks of a rhetorical composition, using stock examples. For the general thoughts, cf. Otho's speech, 15.4-8.

4. Cato and Scipio: M. Porcius Cato, 'of Utica', and Q. Metellus Scipio, consul 52 BC and father-in-law of Pompey, after Pompey's defeat at Pharsalus rallied the remaining Republicans and concentrated them in North Africa; Julius Caesar, after a difficult campaign, defeated Scipio at Thapsus on 6th April 46 BC, and he was killed while trying to flee to Spain. Cato, after ensuring the evacuation of fugitives from Utica to Spain, committed suicide rather than accepting pardon from Caesar. In general see the *African War*, written by one of Caesar's officers and generally published along with Caesar's works.

6. sounded the soldiers and found them in favour of peace: cf. Tac. *H.* II 45. 'The next day the Othonian army's desire was not in doubt, and even those who had been more bellicose were changing their minds'. Tacitus does not give the details of the envoys and the negotiations, nor does he mention Celsus' danger, sections 9-10. Cf. also Dio LXIV 10.2a.

7. Vitellius' army was already on the march: according to Tacitus, *H.* II 45, it had halted on the day of the battle at the fifth milestone (i.e. about $7^1/_2$km) from Bedriacum.

9. the ambush: 7.2-5.

11. Titianus was regretting: cf. Tac. *H.* II 45, 'the envoys were detained for a short while; this caused the army, still not knowing if their request for peace had been accepted, to hesitate'; he does not mention Titianus, or any overt change of mind.

12. others opened the gates: Tac. loc. cit., 'the rampart was opened'; Tacitus then turns to effective scene-painting, probably mostly not based on the 'Common Source'.

13. took the oath: not mentioned by Tacitus, but indispensable.

14.1. its confused and irregular character: Thucydides VII 44.1 is the classic statement of the impossibility of getting a clear description of any major battle.

2. Mestrius Florus: L. Mestrius Florus, consul under Vespasian, between 72 and 75, and a friend of the emperor, Suet. *Vesp.* 22. His earlier career is unknown. For Plutarch in Italy, see Introduction p. 2.
not from choice: cf. Tac. *H.* I 88, 'Otho ordered many of the magistrates and a large proportion of the consulars to accompany him'; Octavian (the later Augustus) had done the same in his war against Antony, *Res Gestae* 25.3, cf. Dio L 11.5.
ancient temple: unidentified, though Hardy's suggestion (ad loc.) that it was that of Castor and Pollux (7.2 note) is appealing.

3. no prisoners were taken: Tac. *H.* II 44, 'in civil wars the captives are not sold for profit'. Dio LXIV 10.3 gives the total killed in all the fighting around Cremona as 40,000, certainly a great exaggeration.

15-17. Otho's last hours and death. See Tac. *H.* II 46-9, with Chilver's notes; Suet. *Otho* 9.3-11.2 and Murison's notes; Dio LXIV 11-15.2[1]; Murison, *Galba, Otho and Vitellius* 131-3, 136-42. It is plain that the 'Common Source' made a feature of Otho's unexpected self-sacrifice, and very likely that there were several other contemporary accounts of the emperor's last days and his suicide; if they were written, or at least published, under the Flavians, they could be expected to make Otho a shining figure to increase the contrast with his successful rival, Vitellius.

15.1. the first news to reach Otho was inconclusive: contrast Tac. *H.* II 46, 'first there was gloomy rumour'; Otho was at Brixellum, about 20 Roman miles (30km) from Bedriacum, 10.1 and note.

eye-witness reports: Tac. loc. cit., 'then fugitives from the battle made clear his cause was lost'; he says nothing about 'wounded' (how would they have reached Brixellum so quickly?), but Suet. *Otho* 10.1, on the authority of his father, writes that 'when a common soldier reported the army's disaster and no one believed him – instead some accused him of lying, others of cowardice, for fleeing from the battle – he fell on his sword before Otho's feet'; cf. the very similar story in Dio LXIV 11, and the variant below, section 3; Tac. *H.* III 54 tells an identical story about a centurion, Julius Agrestis, reporting to Vitellius the true situation after his troops' defeat at Cremona later in 69.

the reaction of the soldiers: Tac. *H.* II 46, the fullest source, claims they urged him to continue the fight, since he still had undefeated forces.

2. not to abandon them: Tac. loc. cit. puts this plea into the mouth of Plotius Firmus, the Praetorian Prefect (colleague of Proculus, 7.6).

3. killed himself: see section 1 and note.

4-8. Otho's speech: Tac. *H.* II 47 and Dio LXIV 13 give similar accounts, but plainly each author has embellished the 'Common Source' with ideas and examples of his own.

6. army from Moesia: Tac. *H.* II 46, 'men sent ahead from Moesia reported the same determination in the approaching army, and that the legions had reached Aquileia'.

Asia, Syria, Egypt and the forces fighting the Jews: see 4.3 and note. 'Asia' presumably is not only the province Asia, which had a negligible garrison, but all of Asia Minor; Egypt was governed by Ti. Julius Alexander, cf. *Galba* 6.1, who struck coins in Otho's name, and was the first governor to proclaim Vespasian emperor, on 1st July 69.

the Senate: cf. Tac. *H.* I 76, which makes many of the same points about the support for Otho.

wives and children: including Vitellius', 5.2-3 and notes.

7. Hannibal or Pyrrhus or the Cimbri: the three great examples of foreign invaders who tried to conquer Rome and were driven out of Italy: Hannibal 218-203 BC, Pyrrhus 280-275 BC, the Cimbri 102-101 BC. Plutarch was to write a *Life* of Pyrrhus, *Lives* of Fabius Maximus and Claudius Marcellus, who fought Hannibal, and of Marius and Sulla, who defeated the Cimbri. His lost *Life* of Scipio may have been about the conqueror of Hannibal, or about his grandson by adoption, Aemilianus. These examples are Plutarch's own; Dio gives quite different ones, and Tacitus none at all.

16.1. told his friends: Tac. *H.* II 48, 'he told them to leave promptly and not exacerbate the victor's anger by delaying'.

he wrote letters: not the usual diplomas (*Galba* 8.5 note), since these lost their validity at the emperor's death (Tac. *H.* II 54).

2. nephew Cocceianus: L. Salvius Otho Cocceianus, son of Otho's brother Titianus, Tac. *H.* II 48, who mentions the same advice; cf. Suet. *Otho* 10.2, who does not there name him. Domitian put him to death for celebrating Otho's birthday, Suet. *Dom.* 10.3.

3. adopt you as my son: not mentioned by any other source.

5. confused shouting: Tac. *H.* II 49, who adds that the soldiers were particularly incensed with Verginius Rufus; Suet. *Otho* 11.1, Dio LXIV 15.1a.

no bland entreaties: for the first time Otho is shown as not currying favour with the soldiers; Tac. loc. cit. agrees, and Suet. loc. cit. implies the same.

17.1. evening: 15th April, the day after the battle, Murison, *Galba, Otho and Vitellius* 92-3.

drank a little water: Tac. *H.* II 49, Suet. *Otho* 11.2.

two swords: or daggers, Tac. and Suet. locc. citt.

put the other under his arm: Tacitus, II 49, and Suetonius, 10.2, first describe how Otho distributed his goods and said farewell to his servants, and then how he chose a dagger, which, according to them, he placed under his pillow and then went to sleep; Plutarch, reversing the order, has to make Otho conceal the dagger. Vitellius later sent it to Colonia Agrippinensis, where he had been hailed emperor, to be dedicated to Mars, Suet. *Vitell.* 10.3.

his servants: Tacitus' account suggests that he gave his money to depart-ing senators, as does Dio's LXIV 15.1a; Suetonius agrees with Plutarch. Plutarch, unlike the other sources, does not mention that Otho burnt all the letters he had which might be compromising.

4. the freedman: this detail, of Otho's concern for the safe departure of the senators, is preserved only by Plutarch, as is his concern for the safety of his freedman. Cf. the fate of Epaphroditus, who helped Nero commit suicide and was later executed by Domitian, since no one who had helped kill an emperor should be allowed to live (Suet. *Nero* 49.3, *Domit.* 14.4).

5. single groan: perhaps inferred by Plutarch from the 'Common Source', which Tacitus and Suetonius seem to follow more closely, *H.* II 49, 'at the groan of the dying man, his freedmen and slaves entered'; *Otho* 11.2, 'they rushed in at the first groan'.

8. built a pyre: Tac. loc. cit., 'his funeral was hurried on, as he had urgently begged, since he feared his head might be cut off and insulted'; Suet. loc. cit., 'as he had instructed, he was quickly buried'; neither explicitly mentions the military honours, but took them for granted.

9. kissed the wound or clasped its hands: the same phrases in Tac. loc. cit., Suet. *Otho* 12.2.

10. then killed themselves: this detail is in all accounts, Tac. and Suet. locc. citt., Dio LXIV 15.1^2.

12. implacable hatred for Vitellius: Vitellius dismissed the Praetorian Guard and replaced them with men from the Rhine legions; the dismissed men thereupon joined the Flavian side. See *Galba* 2.4 note. The legions who had fought for Otho were also embittered against Vitellius, Tac. *H.* II 60, 66-7, 86.

18.1. in its own time: obviously in the lost *Life* of Vitellius.

devoid of pretension: Tac. *H.* II 49, 'For Otho a tomb was constructed, modest and lasting'; cf. Suet. *Vitell.* 10.3.

epitaph: only Plutarch gives the wording; the translation rests on a very probable conjecture to correct the unintelligible manuscript reading.

3. thirty-seven years old: he was born 28th April 32 (Suet. *Otho* 2.1), proclaimed emperor 15th January 69, and committed suicide 16th April 69, so he was near the end of his 37th year, as Tacitus says, loc. cit; Dio is even more precise, 'he lived 37 years less eleven days' (LXIV 15.21); Suet. *Otho* 11.2 wrongly says 'in his 38th year'.

emperor for three months: Suet. loc. cit. 'the 95th day of his rule' (see Murison, ad loc.); Dio loc. cit. 'the 90th day'.

he died more nobly: cf. Tac. *H.* II 50, Suet. *Otho* 12.2, Dio LXIV 15.2a, with similar sentiments.

4. Plotius: 15.2 note; the manuscripts read 'Pollio'.

5. with the exception of Verginius Rufus: Tac. *H.* II 51 tells the same story more briefly and without giving Rufus' reasons; for him, see *Galba* 6 and notes.

6. forced unwelcome decisions: especially by refusing to be proclaimed emperor by them, and by forcing them to swear allegiance to Galba, *Galba* 10 and notes.

7. joined Caecina: Tac. *H.* II 51 gives brief details of the negotiations; cf. Dio LXIV 15.2b.

The ending of the *Otho* is as abrupt as that of the Galba; no doubt Plutarch's *Life* of Vitellius took up the story without a break.

Bibliography

Ancient Sources

Augustus, *RG*: Augustus, *Res Gestae*, Latin text edited with translation and commentary by P. Brunt and J.M. Moore (Oxford, 1967).

Dio: Cassius Dio (Loeb edition).

Diodorus, *History* (Loeb edition).

CIL: *Corpus Inscriptionum Latinarum* (texts, introduction and commentary in Latin).

Hesiod, *Theogony, Works and Days* (Loeb edition).

ILS: *Inscriptiones Latinae selectae* (texts, introduction and commentary in Latin).

Josephus, *Jewish War* and *Jewish Antiquities* (Loeb edition).

Juvenal, *Satires* (Loeb edition, and Penguin translation).

Lactantius, *De Mortibus Persecutorum*, (ed.) J. Moreau (Paris, 1954); (ed.) J. Creed (with English translation and commentary) (Oxford, 1984).

Livy, *History* (Loeb edition).

McCrum, M., and Woodhead A.G., *Select Documents of the Principates of the Flavian Emperors, AD 68-96* (Cambridge, 1961) (texts in the original languages).

Martial, *Epigrams* (Loeb edition).

Philostratus, *Life of Apollonius of Tyana* (Loeb edition).

Pliny, *Ep.*: Younger Pliny, *Letters* (Loeb edition, and Penguin translation).

Pliny, *NH*: Elder Pliny, *Natural History* (Loeb edition).

Pliny, *Pan.*: Younger Pliny, *Panegyric* (Loeb edition).

Plutarch, *Lives* and *Moralia* (Loeb edition).

Polyaenus, *Stratagems* (no modern English translation).

RIC: see Sutherland, in Bibliography.

Seneca: Younger Seneca (Loeb edition).

Strabo, *Geography* (Loeb edition).

Suet.: Suetonius, *Lives* of Augustus, Tiberius, Gaius, Claudius, Nero, Galba, Otho, Vitellius, Vespasian, Titus, Domitian (Loeb edition).

Tac. *A.*, *Agr.*, and *H.*: Tacitus, *Annals*, *Agricola* and *Histories* (Loeb edition, and Penguin translations).

Modern Works Cited

Barrow, R.H., *Plutarch and his Times* (London, 1967).

Berger, A., *Encyclopedic Dictionary of Roman Law* (Philadelphia, 1953).

Bradley, K.R., *Suetonius' Life of Nero: an Historical Commentary* (Brussels, 1978).

Braun, L., 'Galba und Otho bei Plutarch und Sueton', *Hermes* CXX (1992) 90-102.

Braund, D.C., *Augustus to Nero, a Sourcebook on Roman History* (London, 1985).

Buckland, W.W., *The Roman Law of Slavery* (Cambridge, 1908).

Casson, L., *The Ancient Mariners*, 2nd edn (Princeton, 1991).

Chilver, G.E.F., *A Historical Commentary on Tacitus' Histories I and II* (Oxford, 1979).

Clunia I, *Hallazgos monetarios*. II, *La epigrafia de Clunia* (Madrid, 1985, 1987).

Cramer, F.H., *Astrology in Roman Law and Politics* (Philadelphia, 1954).

Crook, J.A., *Consilium principis* (Cambridge, 1955).

———— *Law and Life of Rome* (London, 1967).

Eder, W., *Servitus publica* (Wiesbaden, 1981).

Ehrhardt, C.T.H.R., 'Messalina and the succession to Claudius', *Antichthon* XII (1978) 51-77.

Fabia, P., *Les sources de Tacite dans les Histoires et les Annales* (Paris, 1893).

Georgiadou, A., 'The *Lives of the Caesars* and Plutarch's other *Lives*', *Illinois Classical Studies* XIII (1988) 349-56.

Grant, M., *Nero, Emperor in Revolt* (New York, 1970).

Hainsworth, J.B., 'Verginius and Vindex', *Historia* XI (1962) 86-96.

Haley, E.W. 'Clunia, Galba and the events of 68-69', *Zeitschrift für Papyrologie und Epigraphik* XCI (1992) 159-64.

Hardy, E.G., *Plutarch's Lives of Galba and Otho, with Introduction and Explanatory Notes* (London, 1890).

Hewitt, K.V., 'The coinage of L. Clodius Macer (AD 68)', *Numismatic Chronicle* CXLIII (1983) 64-80.

Jones, C.P., *Plutarch and Rome* (Oxford, 1971).

Kessissoglu, A.I., 'Plutarch V. Galbae 7, 5', *Hermes* CIII (1975) 127-8 (in German).

Levick, B., 'L. Verginius Rufus and the four emperors', *Rheinisches Museum*

CXXVIII (1985) 318-46.

Levick, B., *Claudius* (London, 1990).

MacMullen, R., 'How to revolt in the Roman empire', *Rivista Storica dell'Antichità* XV (1985) 67-76.

Martin, P.-H., *Die anonymen Münzen des Jahres 68 nach Christus* (Mainz, 1974).

Murison, C.L., *Suetonius, Galba, Otho, and Vitellius* (edited with introduction and notes) (London, 1992).

―――― *Galba, Otho and Vitellius: Careers and Controversies* (Hildesheim, 1993).

Ogilvie, R.M., *The Romans and their Gods in the Age of Augustus* (London, 1969).

Oxford Classical Dictionary, 2nd edn (Oxford, 1970).

Parke, H.W., *Greek Mercenary Soldiers from the Earliest Times to the Battle of Ipsus* (Oxford, 1933).

Parker, H.M.D., *The Roman Legions*, 2nd edn by G.R. Watson (Cambridge, 1958).

Salmon, E.T., *Roman Colonization under the Republic* (London, 1969).

Sage, M.M., 'Tacitus' historical works: a survey and appraisal', *Aufstieg und Niedergang der römischen Welt* II 33, 2 (Berlin, 1990) 893-7.

Sherk, R.K., *The Roman Empire, Augustus to Hadrian* (Translated Documents of Greece and Rome) (Cambridge, 1988).

Sherwin-White, A.N., *The Letters of Pliny, A Historical and Social Commentary* (Oxford, 1966).

Sutherland, C.H.V., *The Roman Imperial Coinage* I^2 (London, 1984).

Syme, R., *Tacitus* (Oxford, 1958).

Talbert, R., *The Senate of Imperial Rome* (Princeton, 1984).

Titchener, F.B., 'Critical trends in Plutarch's Roman Lives, 1975-1990', *Aufstieg und Niedergang der römischen Welt* II 33, 6 (Berlin, 1992) 4128-53, esp. 4153.

Warmington, B.H., *Suetonius, Nero* (text with introduction and notes) (Bristol, 1977).

Watson, G.R., *The Roman soldier* (London, 1969).

Webster, G. , *The Roman Imperial Army*, 3rd edn (London, 1985).

Ziegler, K., 'Plutarchos von Chaironeia', Pauly-Wissowa, *Real-enzyklopädie der classischen Altertumswissenschaft* 41.1 (Stuttgart-Waldsee, 1951) 636-962.

Translations of the the Lives

Jacques Amyot (into French) 1559.

Sir Thomas North 1579, reprinted, with introduction by George Wyndham, 1896.

John Dryden 1683-6, revised by Arthur Hugh Clough 1859-60. The translations are by several hands. Dryden himself wrote only the dedication and introduction.

John and William Langhorne 1770.

Aubrey Stewart and George Long 1880-2.

Bernadotte Perrin (Loeb edition, text and translation) 1914-26.

Index of Names and Subjects

Note: Place-names are listed in the form in which they occur in the text, with the ancient or modern equivalent if it also occurs, as: 'Piacenza (Placentia)'. Personal names are also listed in the form in which they occur, as 'Gaius Caesar'. Where this is not the common name, or where ambiguity is possible, cross-reference is given, as: 'Caligula, v. Gaius Caesar'. Apart from subject references (as: 'Galba, reputation for meanness'), references to Galba and Otho are not given for their own *Life*. References are not given for secondary sources, ancient or modern, cited in the Commentary.

tomb, 36, 99; lover of Sporus, 57; early career of, 70; coins struck for, 97; care for his followers, 99

P

Palatine (the imperial residence), 9, 10, 22, 25, 39, 43-4, 76

Palestine, forces of, v. Judaea

Pannonia, forces of, 28, 31, 86, 89, 92

Paris (of Troy), 19

Patrobius, freedman of Nero, 17, 25, 68, 82

Paulinus, v. Suetonius

Paulus, basilica of, v. basilica

Petinus, 17, 67-8

Petronius Turpilianus, 16, 18, 64, 65

Pharsalus, battle of, 33, 95

Piacenza (Placentia), 29, 30, 89

Piso, L. Calpurnius: adopted by Galba, 21; appeals to Palace Guards, 23; death of, 24; head recovered by his wife, 25; his exile, 75; family, 75

Pisonian conspiracy, 39, 40, 49, 56, 63, 64, 70, 71

Plato, 9, 37

Pliny, the Elder, 4

Pliny, the Younger, 4

Plotius Firmus, 36, 91, 97

Plutarch: Intro. passim; *Lives* of Aratus and Artaxerxes, 1; of Augustus and Demosthenes, 1, 2; of Aemilius Paulus and Timoleon, 37; inconsistency, 38; interpretation of events, ibid.; date of *Galba* and *Otho*, 39, 57, 59; *Life* of Nero, 39; conception of biography, 42; difficulty with

Roman names, 42; accuracy, 65, 67, 93; inaccuracies, 72, 75, 77, 78, 79, 85, 89, 90, 95; religiosity, 77; favourable portrayal of Galba, 80; *Life* of Camillus, 83; *Lives* of Scipio and Pyrrhus, 83, 98; dislike of Praetorians, 85, 95; *Lives* of Fabius Maximus, Claudius Marcellus, Marius, Sulla, 98; *Life* of Vitellius, 1, 2, 3, 99

Po, river (Padus), 32, 89, 93, 94

Polybius, his 'pragmatic' history, 42

Polycleitus, 17, 67

Polyphron of Pherae, 9, 38

Pompey (Cn. Pompeius Magnus), 31, 92, 95

Poppaea Sabina, second wife of Nero: her name given to Sporus by Nymphidius, 13; by Nero, 57; married to Otho and shared with Nero, 19; parents, and first marriage of, 70

portents (v. also divination), 21, 22, 28, 75, 87

Praetorian Guard: induced by Nymphidius to proclaim Galba emperor, 10, 40; placed under command of Cornelius Laco, 15; treachery to Galba, 22, 42; called 'mercenaries' by Plutarch, 26, 85; mutinous violence towards Senate, 26, 85; mistrust of Dolabella, 28; insubordination, 29, 89; impatience for battle, 31; cowardice, 33; organization of, 40; support for Vespasian, 42; attached only to emperor, 47; *speculatores* among, 56; prefects of, 40, 61, 85; involved in plots against Nero and Caligula, 63; Roman citizens, 85; re-formed by Vitellius, 99

priesthoods, 26, 83

prisoners, not taken in civil war, 34, 96

procurators, 10, 45, 69

Proculus, Licinius, Othonian commander, 30, 32, 33, 91, 93

Ptolemaeus, astrologer, 22, 76

Pyrrhus of Epirus, 35, 98

Pythian Games, 29, 89

Q

Quintilian, 4

R

Rome: Galba's unpopularity in, 17-18; reaction to Otho's coup, 26, 84; Praetorian riot in, 27, 84; shortage of grain in, 28, 50, 87; capture of, by Flavian forces, 42; by Sulla and Marius, 92; reaction to Nero's death, 13, 56; enthusiasm for presence of emperor, 60; apartment blocks in, 62; controlled by Nero's freedmen, 67

Rubellius Plautus, 44, 61

Rufrius Crispinus, first husband of Poppaea Sabina, 19, 70

S

Sabinus, v. Calvisius; Flavius; Nymphidius

Sage, M., 4

satyrs, 17, 67

Scipio, P. Cornelius (Aemilianus), 25, 82-3

Scipio, P. Cornelius (Africanus), 25, 82-3

Scipio, Q. Metellus, 33, 95

Scribonia, mother of Piso, 22, 75

Secundus, v. Julius

Sempronius Densus, 24, 79

Senate: outlaws Galba, 11; subservience to Nymphidius Sabinus, 13; oath of loyalty to Otho, 25, 81; addressed by Otho, 26; threatened by Praetorian Guards, 26, 85; behind Otho's lines, 35, 98; delegations from, to Vespasian and Galba, 59; imperial power conferred by, 31, 70

Seneca, L. Annaeus, 19, 49, 71

Septimius, 16, 64

Servii, 10, 42-3

Sessorium, 25, 82

Sinuessa, 26, 84

slaves, 55

speeches, invented, 47, 63, 86, 95, 97, 98

Spiculus, 13, 56

'Spoiler' (*legio XXI Rapax*), 32, 94

Sporus, 13, 57

Spurinna, T. Vestricius, Othonian commander, 29, 30, 88, 89

stade, 65

Suetonius, 3

Suetonius Paulinus, Othonian commander: 29; accused of treachery, and deprived of authority, 30, 91; counsels delay, 30-1, 92; unwilling to advance, 32; avoids his defeated troops, 33; career, 88; perhaps ambitious to be emperor, 93

Sulla, L. Cornelius, 31, 92

'Support' (*legio I Adiutrix*), 32, 65, 66, 94

Works of Plutarch Cited

Lives: *Aemilius Paulus* 13.6, 37; *Alexander* 1, 42; *Antony*, 87, 39; *Aratus*, 1; *Artaxerxes*, 1; *Augustus*, 1, 2; *Brutus* 20.5-6, 68; *Caesar*, 68; *Camillus*, 83; *Cato Minor*, 16, 43; *Crassus*, 13, 43; *Demosthenes* 2, 1, 2; *Fabius Maximus*, *Marcellus*, *Marius*, 98; *Nero*, 39; *Nicias* 1.5, 42; *Pelopidas*, 29, 38; *Phocion* 22, 38; *Pyrrhus*, *Scipio*, 83, 98; *Sulla*, 98; *Timoleon*, 37; *Vitellius*, 1, 2, 3

Moralia: 127F, 38; 175C-176C, 38; 181F, 38; 336F, 38; 385B, 1; 501E, 2; 608-12, 2; 678C, 2; 786C, 67; 798-825, 2; Loeb edn vol. XV 17, no. 100, 42

www.ingramcontent.com/pod-product-compliance
Ingram Content Group UK Ltd.
Pitfield, Milton Keynes, MK11 3LW, UK
UKHW031251020325
455690UK00007B/105